Model Essays for IB and A Level Economics

MICROECONOMICS Volume 2

Kelvin Hong

Ang Jun Yang

First Printing: 2020

ISBN 9789811449871

Edventures Pte Ltd

Singapore

www.TheEconomicsTutor.com

Acknowledgments

This work would not have been possible without the help of Jade Chan who helped in drafting and editing the work.

PREFACE

This book answers 20 key examination questions across the entire Microeconomics syllabus and was created to provide students with the ability to excel in their examinations.

Very often, students are unable to provide step-by-step explanations and relevant evaluation points, which are essential to scoring in examinations.

By studying through the model essays provided in this book, students will also be able to better understand the various economic concepts covered in the Microeconomics syllabus. The powerful diagrammatic analyses provided will also train students to illustrate economic concepts logically, and enable them to use such diagrams for analyses in a more effective and concise manner.

The questions are mostly obtained from past IB examination papers. However, they are also very applicable to the A Level examinations.

We hope students will now see great hope in scoring very well for their essay papers.

Kelvin Hong & Ang Jun Yang

CONTENTS

1. Explain the factors which might influence the cross price elasticity of demand between different products. (10)

<u>Introduction</u>

1. Cross Price Elasticity of Demand (XED) measures the responsiveness of the demand for one good to changes in the price of related goods, ceteris paribus.

2. The formula for XED of good A with respect to good B is given by –

$$XED_{AB} = \frac{\% \text{ change in quantity demanded of good A}}{\% \text{ change in price of good B}}$$

<u>Factor 1: Complements or substitutes</u>

1. One factor which influences the XED value between two goods, A and B, is the nature of the relationship between the two goods in question.

2. Complements are goods that are used jointly to satisfy a particular want. For example, cars and petrol are complements, since petrol is necessary in order to have the car function, and thus consumers will purchase both of these goods together in other to satisfy their desire for private transportation.

3. The XED value for complements is negative – a fall in the price of good B would cause an increase in the demand for good A. For example, cheaper petrol would encourage more consumers to purchase cars and switch from other modes of transportation.

4. Referring to the Fig. 1 on the next page, an increase in supply of petrol from S_1 to S_2 causes price to fall from P_1 to P_2. Hence, quantity demanded of petrol increases from Q_1 to Q_2 and as a result, demand for cars increases from D_1 to D_2.

Market for Petrol   **Market for Cars**

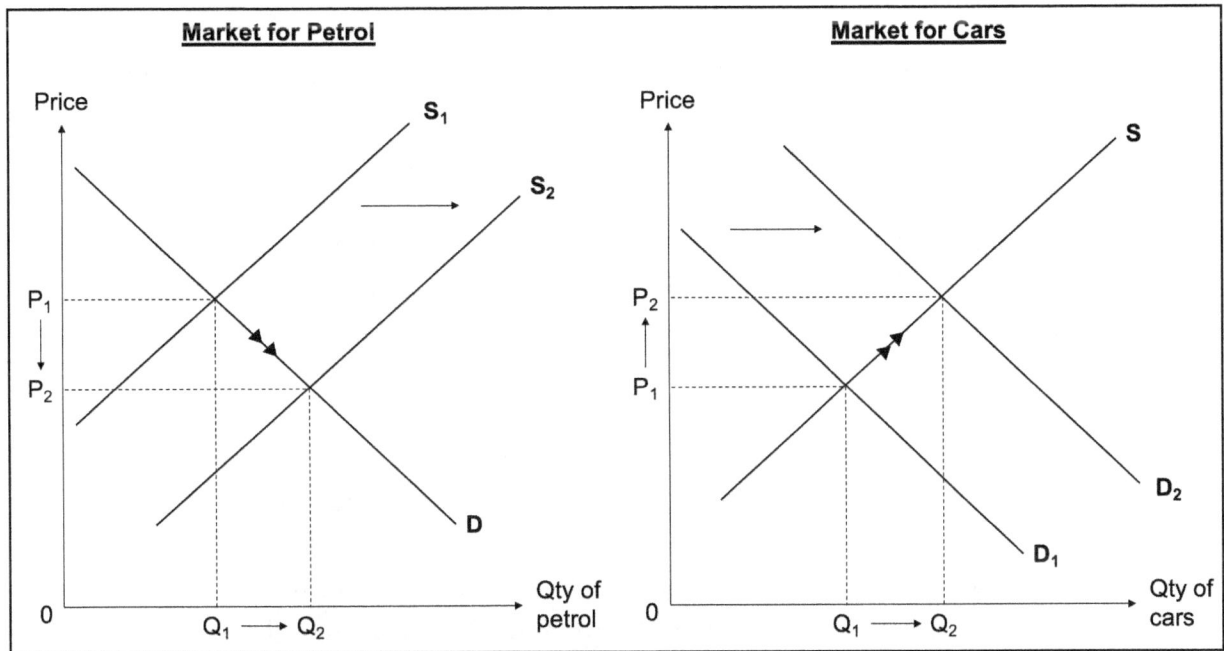

Fig. 1. Complementary Goods, Petrol and Cars.

5. On the other hand, substitutes are alternative products that satisfy similar wants. For example, the soft drinks Coca-Cola and Pepsi are substitutes, since they both satisfy the craving for sugary soda.

6. The XED value for substitutes is positive – a fall in the price of good B would cause a decrease in the demand for good A. For example, a fall in the price of Pepsi would make it a more appealing alternative to Coca-Cola, increasing the quantity demanded for Pepsi while consumers switch from drinking Coca-Cola, thereby causing a decrease in the demand for Coca-Cola.

Factor 2: Closeness of complements/substitutes

1. Another factor which influences XED values is the closeness of the complements and substitutes in question.

2. For example, Coca-Cola and Pepsi are likely to be close substitutes owing to the very similar nature and taste of both products and the same desire which they fulfil. Consequently, the XED of Coca-Cola and Pepsi is likely to be positive and > 1. This means that when the price of Coca-Cola decreases, the demand for Pepsi decreases more than proportionately, as many Pepsi drinkers switch to buying Coca-Cola.

3. On the other hand, while Ferrari cars and Toyota cars are substitutes, they are not close, since they satisfy slightly different desires. Ferrari cars are often purchased more as a status symbol, whereas Toyota cars are purchased just for practical utility. It is not likely that a Ferrari customer would switch to a Toyota, because the latter becomes cheaper. Hence, the XED value for Ferrari and Toyota cars is likely to be positive but small or even near zero in magnitude. A fall in the price of Toyotas would lead to a very slight fall (or not at all) in the demand for Ferraris.

4. Similarly, cars and petrol are likely to be very close complements. Almost all cars need petrol to run, and it is impossible to use the car without first filling it with petrol. Hence, the XED value of these two goods is negative and < -1.

5. On the other hand, tea and creamer are two complementary goods, but are not close complements. While some drink tea with creamer, there are those who prefer their tea plain, without creamer. Hence, the creamer is not strictly necessary for consumers to satisfy their desire for tea, thereby causing the XED for these two goods to be negative but > -1. This means that when the price of tea decreases, the demand for creamer increases less than proportionately.

2. Using a price ceiling diagram, analyse the impact a maximum price might have on the market for food. (10)

Introduction

1. A price ceiling, is a legally established maximum price below the free-market price (Pe). Producers are not allowed by law to sell the good in question at a price above Pmax.

2. For example, the Venezuelan government has recently imposed price ceilings on a wide variety of staple food products, such as bread, which has a maximum price of US$ 0.20 per loaf. This was done with the intention of making food more affordable to low-income groups.

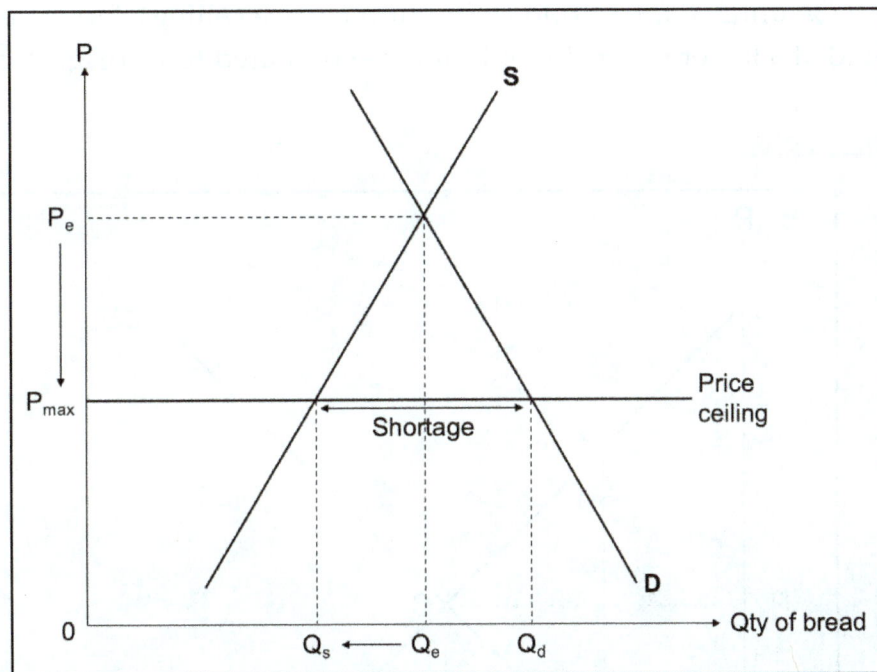

Fig. 2. Price Ceiling imposed in the Market for Bread.

Explanation of Policy

1. In the absence of government intervention, the free market transacts at Qe, with an equilibrium price of Pe, as determined by the intersection of demand and supply.

2. However, following the imposition of a price ceiling Pmax, a shortage of Qd – Qs arises.

3. As the price of bread has decreased, the quantity demanded has increased from Qe to Qd as per the law of demand. With prices falling, with a given income, consumers can now buy more units of the good, causing the real income of consumers to rise, incentivising them to purchase more loaves of bread (income effect). Furthermore, as the price of bread falls, consumers switch from purchasing more expensive food substitutes to purchasing bread instead (substitution effect).At the same time, as the price of bread falls, the quantity supplied decreases from Qe to Qs. This is because the decreased price leads to a lower profit margin for producers of bread, reducing their incentive to produce, thus causing quantity supplied to fall.

4. A permanent shortage thus occurs.

5. Consequently, only Qs units of bread is sold on the market, which is less than the original Qe units of bread sold (without the price ceiling). However, this bread is now sold at a lower unit price of Pmax, as compared to Pe originally.

Analysis of surplus

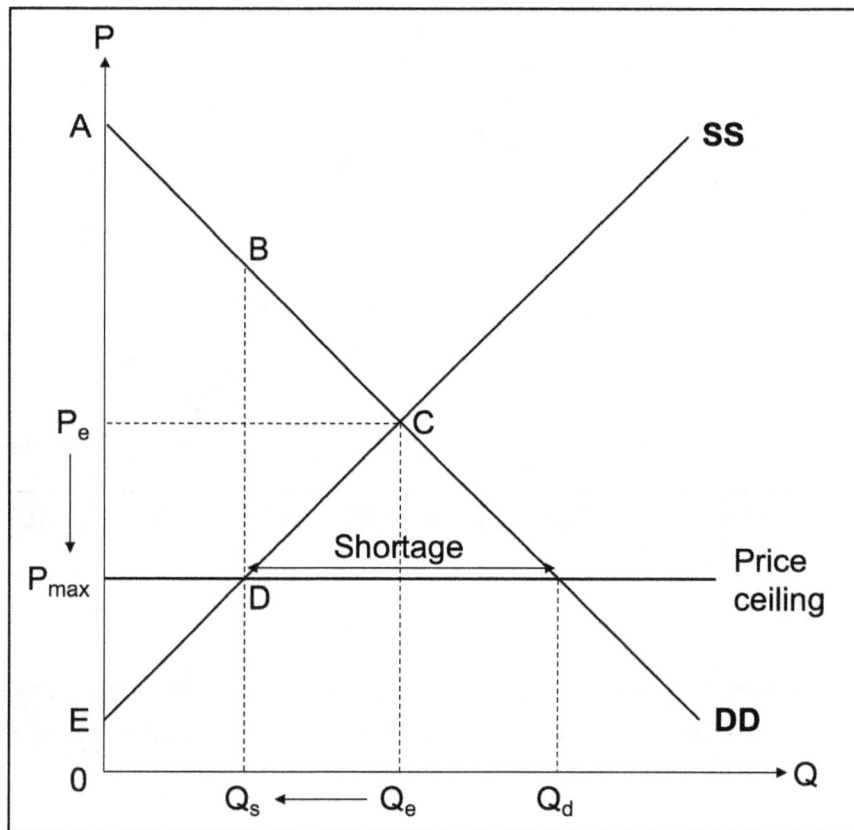

Fig. 3. Price Ceiling Surplus Analysis.

5

1. As a result of the policy, the Producer Surplus (PS) would decrease. This is because the bread producers are now only able to sell fewer loaves of bread, and at a decreased price too. The original PS is represented by area PeCE while the new PS is reduced to area PmaxDE.

2. However, the effect on Consumer Surplus (CS) is ambiguous. On one hand, CS increases as consumers can now purchase bread at a reduced price. On the other hand, CS decreases as consumers are able to purchase fewer loaves of bread. Diagrammatically, there is both an area gain in CS and an area loss in CS, and CS changes from area PeAC to area ABDPmax. The overall effect on CS is uncertain, and depends on the Price Elasticity of Supply (PES) of the good concerned.

3. Should the supply for the good be price inelastic, the imposition of the price ceiling would cause less-than-proportionate decreases in the quantity supplied of the good. As a result, consumers would benefit more from the lowered prices, than they would be harmed by the shortages of the good. Consequently, the net change in CS is positive. The converse holds true for goods whose supply is price elastic.

4. As for society there will be a net welfare loss as a result of this policy. The welfare loss area is represented by the area BCD, and demonstrates the overall losses in CS and PS that are not transferred to another party. Hence, this represents the deadweight welfare loss due to the policy. This assumes that the free market was originally producing at the socially-optimal level of output prior to the policy being implemented.

5. Furthermore, this could facilitate the formation of black markets where food prices are much higher than the original free market equilibrium. As there will be consumers who are unable to obtain the food, but see a dire need for food and would thus be willing to pay higher prices, black markets would form and food may actually become less affordable overall.

3. Explain two factors that might give rise to internal economies of scale for a firm. (10)

Introduction

1. Internal Economies of Scale (IEOS) are the cost savings enjoyed by a firm due to the expansion of the firm itself.

Factor 1: Technical IEOS

1. Specialisation and division of labour: This allows workers to increase their productivity, hence reducing unit costs. By allocating workers to specific tasks, workers can gain knowledge and skills through repetition, hence increasing output per worker per hour. For example, Henry Ford adopted specialisation to assemble the Ford Model T Car, which allowed Ford to increase car production by 8 times using the same number of workers.

2. Indivisibility of factor inputs: Firms with larger output are able to spread out the costs of large machinery which help in enhancing productivity through automation. Large machinery are often too costly for small firms to invest in but upon expansion, the firm might find it viable to purchase the machinery as these fixed costs are spread out over a larger output, lowering per unit costs.

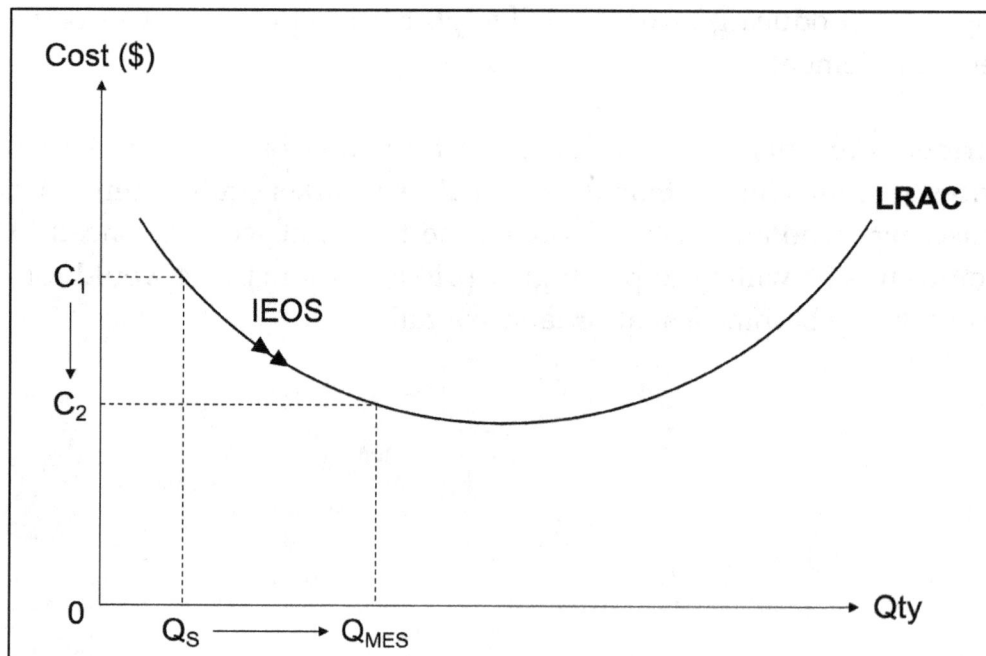

Fig. 4. Q_{MES} represented on the LRAC curve.

3. Referring to Fig. 4 on the previous page, when output is increased from Q_S to Q_{MES}, the average cost decreases from C_1 to C_2.

4. Q_{MES} represents the Minimum Efficient Scale. It is the lowest level of output where the lowest long run average costs (C_2) are achieved.

Factor 2: Marketing IEOS

1. Bigger firms often buy their inputs in bulk. These bigger firms also enjoy larger bargaining power due to their larger market power. Producers of these inputs, eager to secure these bulk orders, might agree to discounts (preferential treatment). Hence, the firm's unit cost of production is lowered.

2. Furthermore, when large firms engage in advertising, the fixed cost is spread over a larger output. Hence, the advertising cost per unit output is lowered.

3. For example, supermarkets like NTUC Fairprice, Cold Storage and Giant purchase all their groceries in much larger quantities as compared to neighbourhood provision stores. Hence, these supermarkets enjoy larger bargaining power and are able to negotiate for lower prices.

4. Explain why some firms might choose the goal of profit maximisation while others might choose to adopt satisficing behaviour. (10)

Goal of profit maximisation

1. Typically, firms are assumed to be profit-maximising since firms exist to earn profits and maximising its profits will mean maximising the income of its shareholders and enabling them to enjoy higher utility from consuming more goods and services.

2. Profits is the difference between the total revenue received from selling the good and the total cost incurred from producing the good.

3. A firm can maximise its profits by producing the amount of output whereby marginal cost = marginal revenue (MC = MR), and when MC is rising and with price determined by the demand curve.

4. Marginal cost is the additional cost incurred by the firm to produce an additional unit of good. Marginal revenue is the additional revenue gained by the firm from the sale of an additional unit of good.

5. When MC < MR, marginal profits can be gained since the additional revenue for every additional unit of output is larger than the additional cost incurred from produced every extra unit of output. Hence, as long as MC < MR, the firm will continue to produce the good as there are additional profits to be earned, and vice versa.

6. The firm will hence produce its last unit of good where MC = MR and there are no additional profits to be captured.

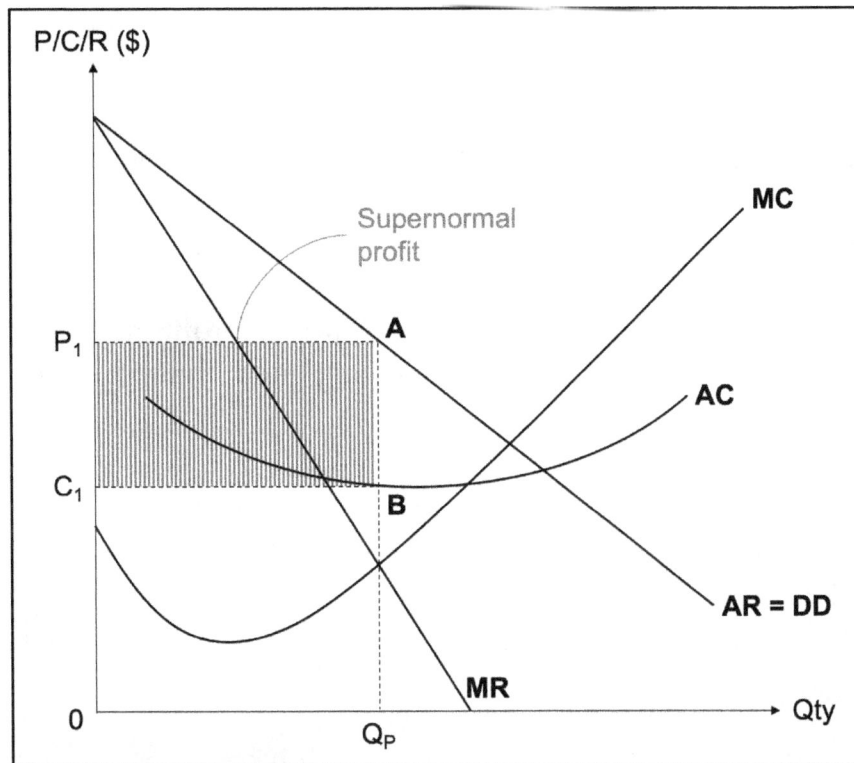

Fig. 5. Profit-Maximising Firm producing Supernormal Profits.

7. As seen from Fig. 5 above, at Q_1 where MC = MR and at P_1, the firm is able to maximise profits. Total revenue is measured by the area $0P_1AQ_1$ and total cost is measured by the area $0C_1BQ_1$. Hence, supernormal profits are represented by the shaded area P_1ABC_1 (total revenue minus total cost).

Satisficing behaviour

1. However, some firms choose instead to adopt profit satisficing behaviour, which is to achieve minimum acceptable levels of profits.

2. Principal-agent problem: Often, in large companies with many levels of employees, ownership and management is separate.

3. Furthermore, each stakeholder has different objectives. Shareholders want maximum profits; employees, including managers, want high wages, promotions, job security and other personal welfare benefits.

4. Managers thus aim for a profit level which can keep shareholders satisfied, instead of the highest possible profit level. This means that managers avoid the increased risks and pressures associated with aggressive policies to increase revenue or cut costs.

10

5. For example, a Manager may not demote certain poor-performing staff in order to maintain good personal relationships with them.

6. Secondly, due to imperfect information, it is hard for a business to pinpoint their precise profit maximising output, as they cannot accurately calculate marginal revenue and marginal cost as well as determine demand.

7. Thus, a firm might look to just add a satisfactory profit margin on top of average cost – this is known as "cost-plus pricing" and thus choosing only to profit satisfice.

5. Explain the conditions necessary for firms in oligopolistic markets to engage in price discrimination. (10)

Introduction

1. Price Discrimination is the selling of the same good at different prices for reasons not due to cost differences.

Condition 1: The firm must be a price setter

1. Oligopolistic markets are characterised by a few large firms that dominate the market. These firms certainly possess a significant degree of market power, as they are able to restrict their output to charge higher prices and vice versa.

2. This is especially so in the case where Oligopoly markets have differentiated goods, as these differences allow firms to increase prices without losing all their market share.

3. For example, in the Singapore market for movie shows, there are only a small number of cinema operators such as Golden Village, Cathay and Shaw. These cinema operators possess large market shares and have the ability to set their own prices.

Condition 2: PED must be different for different consumers

1. Various groups of consumers must have different demand schedules.

2. Consider two differently-priced goods, A and B. For consumers with higher incomes, the demand for the more-expensive good A will likely be relatively price inelastic compared to consumers with lower incomes. As the greater the proportion of a person's income spent on a good, the more price elastic the demand will be, ceteris paribus.

3. Firms must be able to identify the consumers with different PEDs and charge a higher price in the market where demand is more price inelastic and a lower price where demand is more price elastic.

4. Total Revenue (TR) of the company could be increased by shifting output from the market with relatively inelastic demand (market A) to the market with relatively elastic demand (market B). The reduction in revenue from market A is more than compensated by the increase in revenue from market B since the Marginal Revenue (MR) of the last unit sold in market A < MR of last unit sold in market B.

5. For example, in the market for movie shows, students/senior citizens and adults have different ticket prices. Even though they consume the same good (ie. same movie seat, same movie screen), students and senior citizens pay a lower price as compared to adults.

6. This is due to the difference in price elasticity of demand (PED) for students/senior citizens as compared to adults.

7. Adults have higher incomes and thus movie tickets take up a lower proportion of their income. This is in contrast to students/senior citizens with relatively lower incomes. Hence, the magnitude of PED is likely to be < 1 for adults while $|PED|$ is likely to be > 1 for students/senior citizens.

Condition 3: Firm must be able to prevent market seepage at little or no cost

1. The firm must be able to prevent the resale of goods between markets (with minimal additional costs).

2. Otherwise, consumers can purchase goods in the cheaper market and resell it in the more expensive market, hence removing the firm's ability to price discriminate successfully.

3. In the context of cinema shows, before purchasing tickets with discounted rates (student/senior citizen), customers are required to show their identity card to prove their eligibility.

4. Also, there are staff stationed outside cinema doors to check the tickets. This prevents adults from using student/senior citizen tickets to gain entry into the theatre. Hence, market seepage is prevented.

6. Discuss whether price will always be lower and output will always be higher in perfect competition compared to monopoly. (15)

Introduction

1. A firm is considered a monopoly if it is the single seller of a good.

2. As a result, the degree of substitutability is very low and the demand for the good is highly price inelastic.

3. There are high barriers to entry and exit (BTE) within the market. These prevent the entry of new firms, thereby strengthening the monopoly firm's market power.

4. On the other hand, there are infinite number of buyers and sellers in a perfect competition (PC) market structure. Each producer has a very small share of the total market output and is too insignificant to affect total market supply and hence market price.

5. The good being sold in a PC market is assumed to be homogeneous, which means that all goods produced by various firms are perfect substitutes of each other. The demand for a firm's good is thus perfectly price elastic.

6. There are no BTEs in PC. There is free entry and exit of firms.

Thesis: Price always lower and output always higher in PC

1. As the only seller of the good, a monopoly enjoys significant market power and is hence a price-setter.

2. Conversely, firms in PC are price-takers due to an infinitely large number of sellers and assuming all goods to be homogeneous.

3. Monopolies face a downward-sloping demand curve which is also the market demand curve since the single firm constitutes the entire industry (demand curve is also the AR curve).

4. In a PC market, the price of the good is determined at the market level by forces of demand and supply. PC firms, as price-takers, can only charge consumers the market price.

5. Both PC firms and monopolists are profit-maximising and will produce up to the point where MC = MR and where MC is increasing.

6. The monopolist charges consumers the highest price they are willing and able to pay at this output.

7. Referring to Fig. 6 below, the monopolist may price its product at P_M, whereas in a PC market, the market price (determined by the intersection of SS_{PC} and DD_{PC}) is lower at P_{MC}.

8. Additionally, output is higher in PC (Q_{PC}) as compared to monopoly (Q_M).

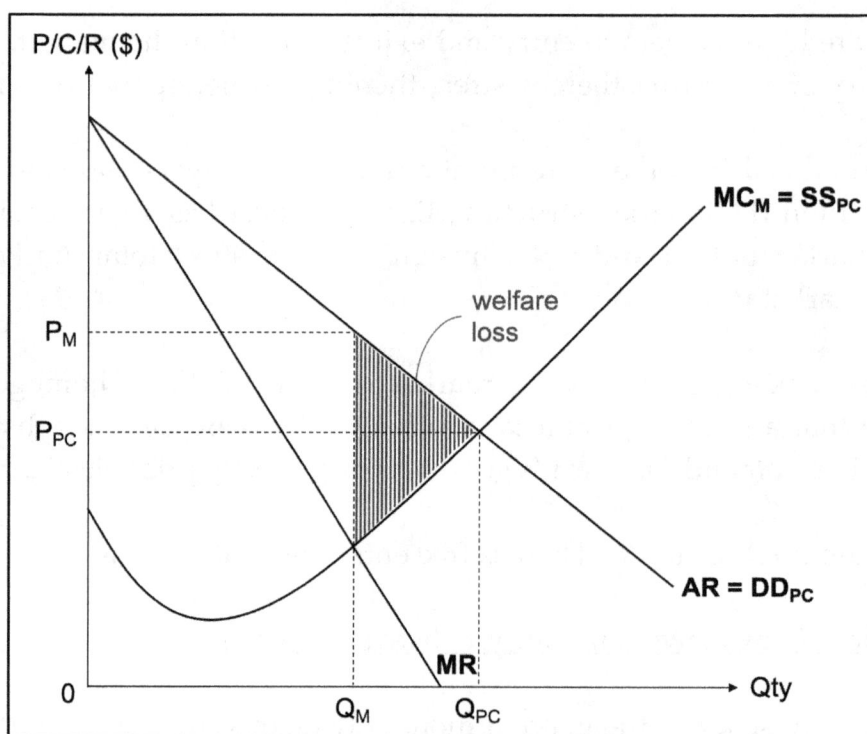

Fig. 6. PC firm producing at lower P and higher Q.

<u>Anti-Thesis 1: Price lower and output higher in monopoly due to IEOS</u>

1. A monopoly firm produces much larger output as compared to individual firms in perfect competition and operates on a much larger scale.

2. Hence, monopolies are able to reap internal economies of scale (IEOS). IEOS is defined as the cost savings enjoyed by a firm are due to the expansion of the firm itself.

3. For example, monopolies could exploit technical IEOS through specialisation and division of labour. As workers gain knowledge and skills through repetition, their productivity increase and output per worker hour increases.

4. Hence, monopolies are able to lower their unit cost of production and their marginal cost (MC_M) curve would be lower than the PC market supply curve (SS_{PC}). (refer to Fig. 7)

5. Furthermore, monopolists are able to earn supernormal profits in the long run. Hence, they have the ability to engage in R&D such as process innovation.

6. Monopolists are hence able to discover new production methods which are more efficient and will lower their MC.

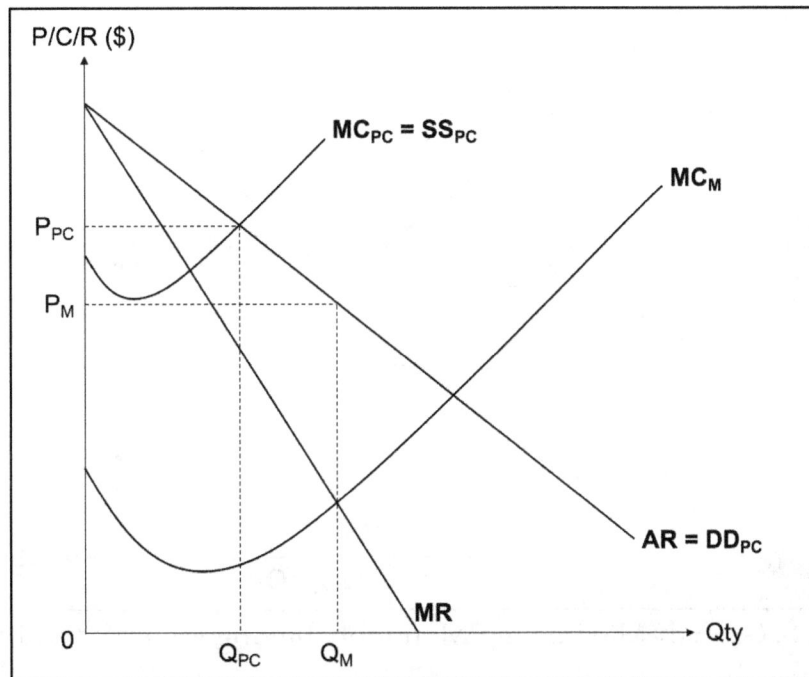

Fig. 7. Monopolist's IEOS leading to lower P and higher Q.

7. Referring to Fig. 7 above, at the profit maximising output level (MC = MR), monopolist may charge a lower price (P_M) than that in a PC (P_{MC}). Also, output increases from Qs to Q1.

Anti-Thesis 2: Price lower and output higher in monopoly due to alternative objectives

1. Moreover, not all monopoly firms will pursue a goal of profit-maximisation. Some may pursue alternative objectives such as growth-maximisation through internal expansion, mergers or acquisitions.

2. A growth-maximising monopoly could choose to produce at break-even output and price, which is where AR = AC, making only normal profits.

3. Hence, the firm could produce an output which is greater and a price that is lower than that of a PC market.

4. As seen in Fig. 8, a firm pursuing for growth-maximisation will produce at output Q_1 which is higher than Q_{MC} and price P_1 which is lower than price P_{MC} in a PC market structure.

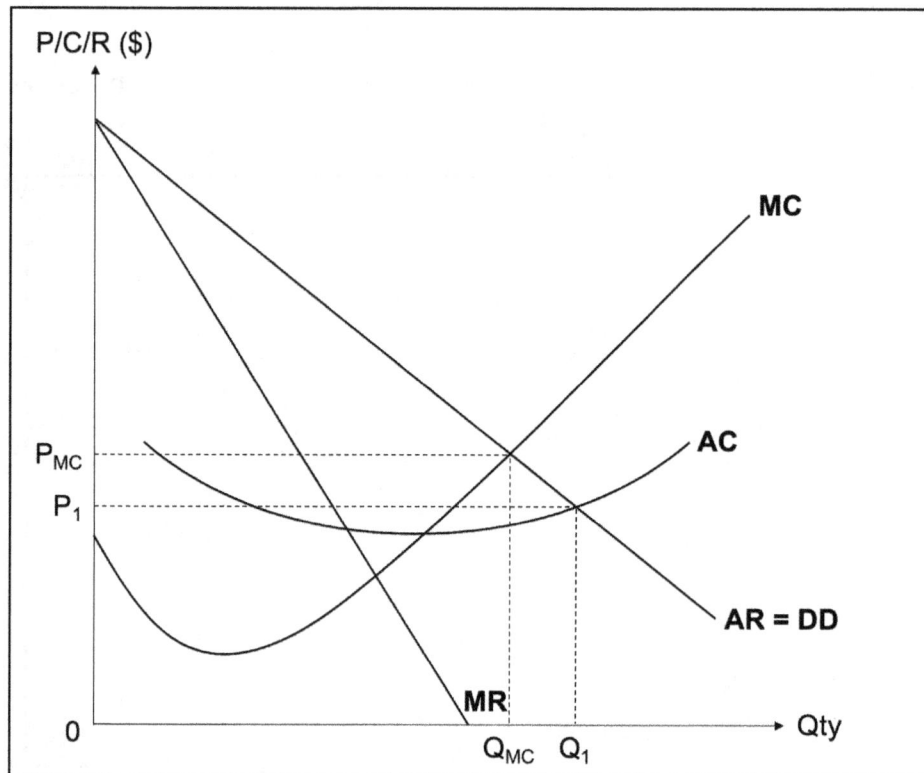

Fig. 8. Growth-Maximising Monopoly having lower P and higher Q.

Anti-Thesis 3: Price not always lower and output not always higher in PC due to highly contestable market

1. In a contestable market, a monopolist is forced to behave like a competitive firm.

2. A contestable market is one that is extremely easy to enter and very low cost to exit from the market. There are low sunk costs, which means there are no barriers to entry.

3. If a monopolist faces no threat of competition (ie. a market with low contestability), it will continue to charge high prices by restricting its output.

17

4. However, in a contestable market, the monopolist is incentivised to keep its prices low and produce more efficiently to protect its market share from potential competitors.

5. Failing to do so would invite new firms to enter the market, eroding the monopolist's market share.

6. Hence, in the case of a contestable market, prices and output in a monopoly might be similar to a PC market.

<u>Conclusion</u>

1. In general, prices will not always be lower and output higher in PC than monopoly. It depends on multiple factors such as the extent of process innovation and the success rate. However, it is unlikely for a pure monopolist to engage in process innovation as there is a lack of incentives in doing so. Monopolists might prefer to keep the supernormal profits and not take the risk as engaging in R&D is considered as a sunk cost.

2. Also, it much depends on how extensive are the IEOS available. If IEOS is significant due to the nature of production, MC might be very much lower for monopoly compared to PC.

3. Lastly, it depends on the degree of contestability of the market. In a highly contestable market, monopolies would behave as a competitive firm to protect their market share.

7. Explain the problems to society arising from monopoly power. (10)

<u>Key problem 1: Allocative Inefficiency (Market Failure)</u>

1. The socially optimal amount of where allocative efficiency is achieved occurs when Price = Marginal Cost (P = MC). This means that society's valuation of the last unit of good is equal to the additional cost of producing that good.

2. Referring to Fig. 9 below, firms being profit-maximising, will produce up to the point where Marginal Cost = Marginal Revenue (MC = MR). This corresponds to the output Q1 where $P_e > P_{PC}$ due to their downward sloping demand and hence MR curve.

3. At this profit-maximising output Qe, there is an underproduction of the good as compared to the socially optimal output (Q_{PC}).

4. This misallocation of resources represents market failure as society's welfare could be further increased if the firm were to increase output till the socially optimal output (Q_{PC}).

5. There is allocative inefficiency and a deadweight welfare loss (shaded area as indicated in Fig. 9) is hence incurred.

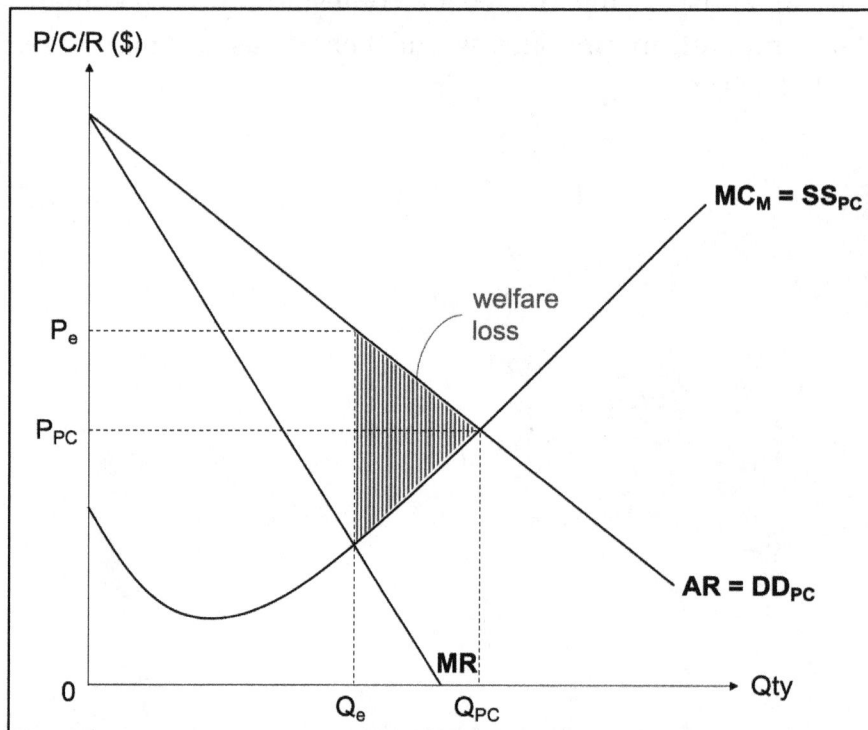

Fig. 9. Under-Production by Monopoly leading to Market Failure.

Key problem 2: Productive Inefficiency

1. Firms with monopoly power tend to be complacent as they are able to earn large supernormal profits even in the long run. They may become organisationally slack, incurring unnecessary costs and hence X-inefficient and produce at a point above the ATC curve.

2. Referring to Fig. 10 below, at output Q_1, cost-efficient firms would produce at its lowest possible average cost, C_1. However, an X-inefficient firm would produce at C_X, a cost higher than C_1.

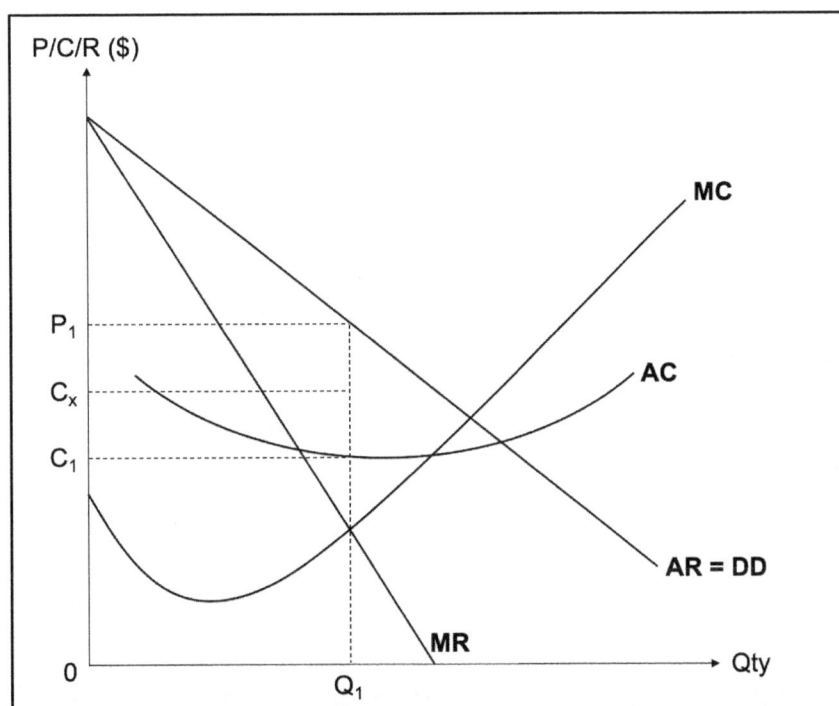

Fig. 10. X-inefficient Firm Producing at a Higher Avg Cost.

3. Furthermore, these firms are already not productively efficient from society's point of view as they are not producing at the minimum point of the ATC curve.

Key problem 3: Income Inequality and Inequity

1. Market dominance may worsen inequity due to the high barriers to entry which impede the entry of new firms. Market power is concentrated in the hands of a few dominant firms which allow them to earn huge supernormal profits even in the long run.

2. Consumers pay high prices while very high incomes are earned by the owners of these firms. This leads to a concentration of income in the hands of a few and further exacerbates income inequality.

3. Furthermore, firms might engage in price discrimination which will further transfer consumer surplus to producer surplus.

4. Taking first degree price discrimination as an example, the firm charges consumers the maximum price they are willing to pay for the good. Consumer surplus is entirely transferred to the producers who will enjoy even higher incomes.

8. Explain two reasons why a government might want to subsidise a good or service. (10)

Introduction

1. A subsidy refers to a payment made by the government to firms for producing a given good.

2. Governments might implement a subsidy to achieve microeconomic goals of efficiency and equity.

Reason 1: To encourage consumption of merit goods (Allocative Efficiency)

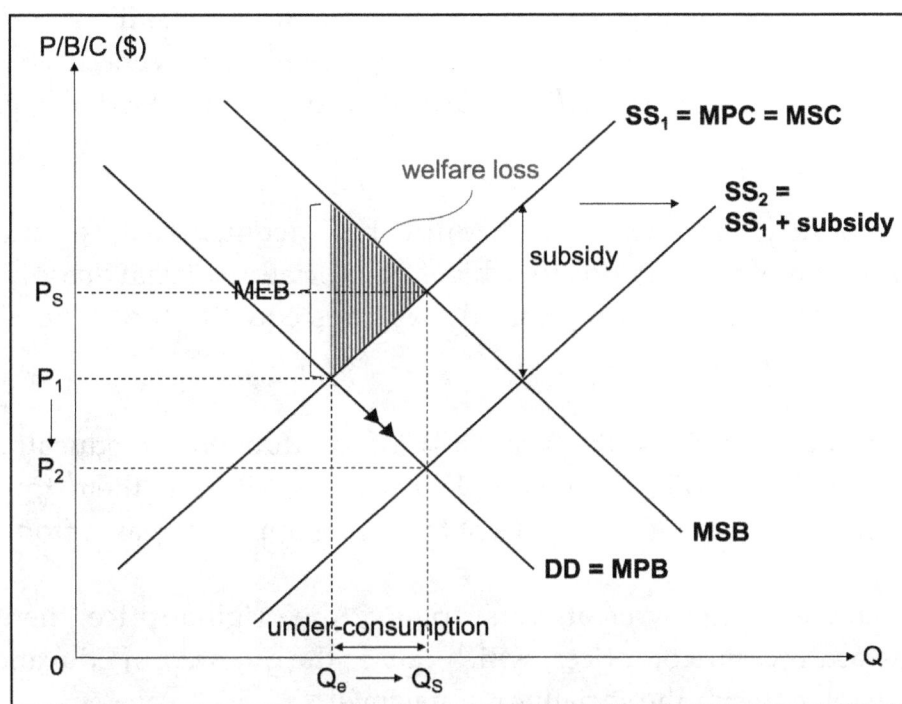

Fig. 11. Subsidy to Increase Consumption of Merit Good.

1. Merit goods refer to goods that are deemed socially-desirable by the government and would be under-consumed if left to the free market. This is usually due to the positive externalities of consumption they generate. Positive externalities refer to spillover benefits that impact third-parties other than the consumer or producer of the good.

2. The Marginal Social Benefit (MSB) exceeds the Marginal Private Benefit (MPB) at each and every quantity, the difference being the Marginal External Benefit (MEB).

3. Referring to Fig. 11 on the previous page, the free market would transact at Qe, where MPB equals to the Marginal Private Cost (MPC).

4. However, this is less than the socially-optimal quantity Qs, where MSB equals to the Marginal Social Cost (MSC). At Qe, MSB > MSC. This means that for each additional unit of the good consumed, the additional benefit to society is greater than the additional cost to society. An increase in consumption beyond Qe would thus increase societal welfare.

5. Hence, there is an under-consumption by the amount Qs − Qe, with a corresponding welfare loss to society as indicated in Fig 11.

6. Higher Education is an example of a merit good. This is because consuming higher education leads to a more well-trained and high-skilled workforce, which drives higher rates of economic growth, benefitting even those who did not consume higher education (3rd parties) through increased job prospects and wages, etc.

7. Consequently, governments would be incentivised to encourage the consumption of merit goods to achieve the socially optimal amount. One way to do so would be to provide a subsidy which is equal to the value of the MEB, as shown in Fig. 11.

8. The subsidy decreases the unit cost of production of education providers, increasing their profit margins and hence incentivising them to supply more. Therefore, the Marginal Private Cost falls and supply increases from SS_1 to SS_2.

9. The increase in supply creates a surplus at the original price, thereby placing a downward pressure on prices, which causes the quantity of education consumed to increase, towards the socially-optimal level.

10. The ideal subsidy would be one whereby the subsidy per unit equals to MEB, which would lead the market to produce at the socially-optimal level.

11. Therefore, governments might seek to impose a subsidy to encourage the consumption of merit goods.

Reason 2: For Equity

1. Another reason why governments might implement a subsidy would be to ensure equity. For example, the US government gives its local farmers a wide variety of subsidies, such as on corn (at US$ 1.95 a bushel) and on rice (at US$ 6.50 a hundredweight).

2. As food is a fundamental necessity, all households would have to spend money purchasing food. High food prices place a severe financial strain on low-income households, for whom a large proportion of income is already spent on daily necessities. Food prices increasing any further might significantly compromise the quality of life experienced by these low-income earners, resulting in inequity.

3. Therefore, to safeguard the interests of these low-income households, the government could implement a food subsidy.

4. This allows the farmers to reduce their unit cost of production and increase their profit margins. Hence, this allows the supply of food to increase from S_1 to S_2. Consequently, this creates a surplus at the original price P_1, placing a downward pressure on prices towards P_2, which therefore make food more affordable to the benefit of low-income earners, thereby improving equity.

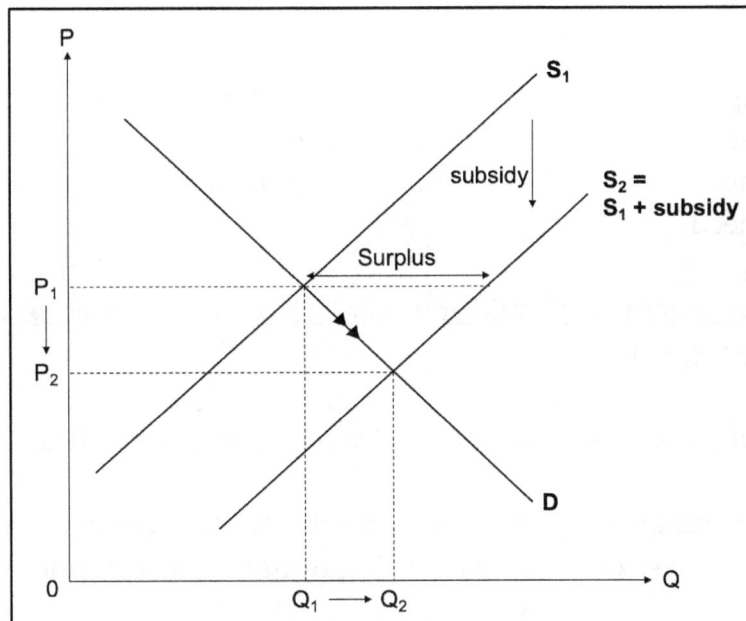

Fig. 12. Subsidy to Lower Food Prices for Low-Income Households.

5. It also helps the farmers by increasing their income and this further improves equity since farmers are often part of the lower segment as well.

9. Discuss whether governments should intervene in housing markets. (15)

Introduction

1. Housing is considered to be a basic necessity and is also often regarded as a merit good.

2. A merit good refers to a good that is deemed socially desirable by the government and would be under-consumed if left to the free market.

Thesis 1: The government should intervene for equity reasons

1. Firstly, the government should intervene in the housing market to lower house or rent prices, should it be deemed that housing prices are unaffordable for the poor.

2. This is especially true for urban metropolises, such as Hong Kong, where the house price-to-income ratio is 18:1 -- the median home price is eighteen times the median annual income. This would make houses very unaffordable for those working low-income jobs far below the median, for whom the ratio might be even higher.

3. As housing is considered a basic human need, and the free market allocates resources not in accordance of need but dollar votes (tied to the ability to pay), the government should intervene on grounds of equity so that even the poor can fulfil this need.

Thesis 2: The government should intervene to correct market failure due to positive externalities generated

1. The consumption of housing generates positive externalities.

2. Positive externalities of consumption refer to the benefits to third parties (other than the consumer or producer) arising from the consumption activity.

3. The free market for housing transacts at Qe, where the Marginal Private Cost (MPC) is equal to the Marginal Private Benefit (MPB). This means that the last unit of housing consumed generates as much benefit for the consumer, as it cost the producer to supply that unit of housing.

4. However, there is a Marginal External Benefit (MEB) arising from the consumption activity which the consumers and producers ignore. This MEB causes a divergence between the MPB and the Marginal Social Benefit (MSB), such that MSB > MPB at each and every quantity.

5. In this case, the MEB involves the societal improvements that result when one has proper housing - namely, reduced rate of homelessness, leading to a more pleasant environment for the general public and reduces incidence of the spread of contagious illness due to lack of poor sanitation.The socially optimal level of consumption is at Qs, where MSB equals to the Marginal Social Cost (MSC). Consequently, the free market under-consumes housing by the amount Qs – Qe.

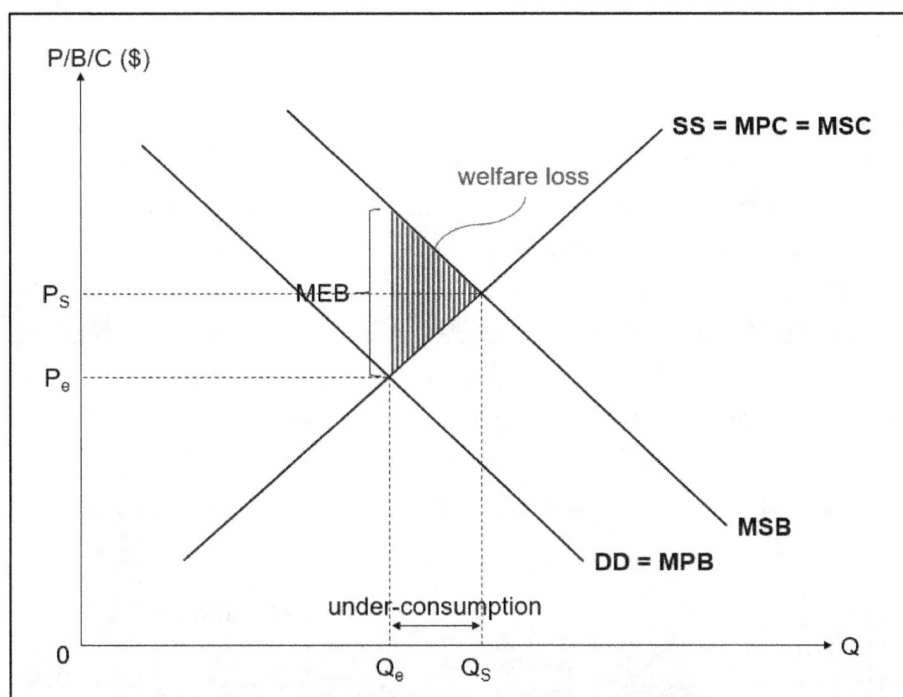

Fig. 13. Positive Externalities of Consumption in the Housing Market.

6. Too few resources are being allocated to housing, and the free market has failed in attaining allocative efficiency.

7. Consequently, given this market failure, the government should be incentivised to step in and correct the issue, with policies designed to increase the consumption of housing up to the socially-optimal level. In doing so, the government is able to ensure that societal welfare is maximised.

Anti-Thesis 1: Government should not intervene in certain cases

1. In highly developed and affluent economies where homeownership rates are high and house prices are affordable, there is little reason for the government to intervene.

2. One prominent example would be Singapore, which has a low poverty rate and a high real income per capita. Singaporeans already have a strong homeownership culture, with a 91.2% homeownership rate.

3. Under such circumstances, where the consumption of housing is evidently high and house prices are affordable to the masses, the government has little incentive to intervene in the housing market.

4. In fact, continued government intervention in such a scenario could lead to over-consumption of housing. Where government policies have pushed house prices too low and driven consumption rates up, housing could be over-consumed, causing a corresponding welfare loss to society.

5. This is as outlined in Fig. 14 below. Assuming policies designed to increase consumption such as the large subsidy as shown below would result in an over-production of houses with a welfare loss to society.

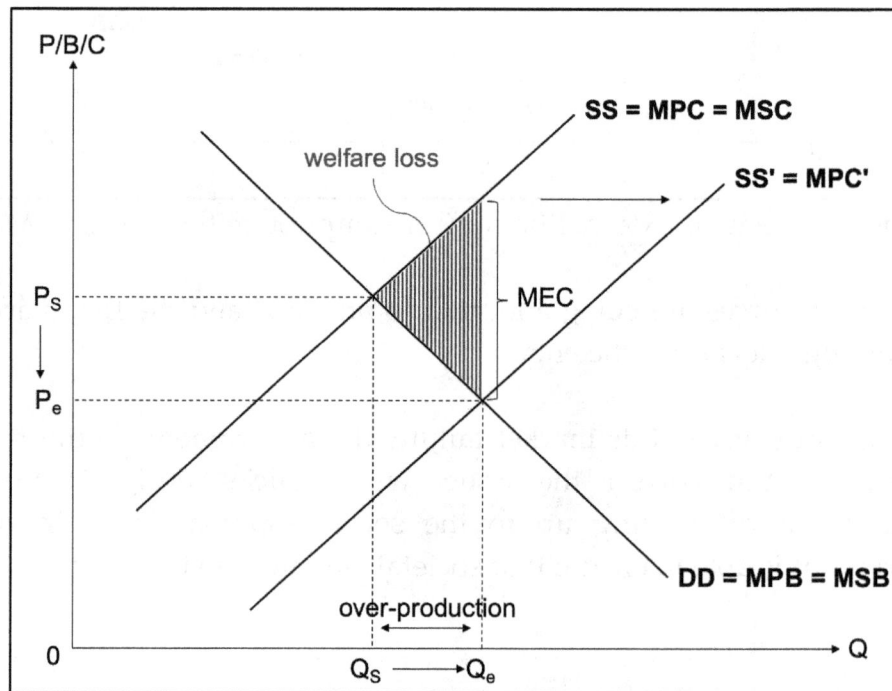

Fig. 14. Government Intervention leading to Market Failure.

6. Similarly, even if there was under-consumption to begin with, as the government introduces policies to encourage consumption of housing, it might still end up with the over-consumption of housing. Governments face information failure and might be unable to accurately estimate the MEB, resulting in an over-subsidy and hence over-consumption.

Anti-Thesis 2: Government should not intervene due to the opportunity cost

1. Various policies that the government could use to intervene in housing markets would incur a high opportunity cost.

2. For example, the government might consider a subsidy, designed to lower prices and increase consumption (correcting the market failure). However, these funds used to finance the subsidy could have been put to better uses, such as to correct more severe under-consumption in other markets such as healthcare.

3. Overall, societal welfare could have been higher if greater resources were allocated to healthcare than housing.

Anti-Thesis 3: Government should not intervene due to policy drawbacks

1. Some policies which the government might use to intervene could carry severe consequences. These consequences could be more severe than the problem the government originally intended to fix.

2. For instance, a price ceiling on housing designed to make it more affordable could instead result in a severe shortages instead, as seen in Fig. 15 on the next page. Without government intervention, the free market equilibrium occurs at output Qe and price Pe. However, after the implementation of a price ceiling, the maximum price is Pmax and there is now a shortage of Qs – Qd.

3. This could drive up homelessness rates as people are unable to purchase houses. A black market for housing could also result, which would not be under the purview of government regulations, and could therefore result in unsafe and even more expensive living conditions.

4. Alternatively, the government might consider a scheme of direct provision, where the government builds and sells public housing at the appropriate price and quantity required.

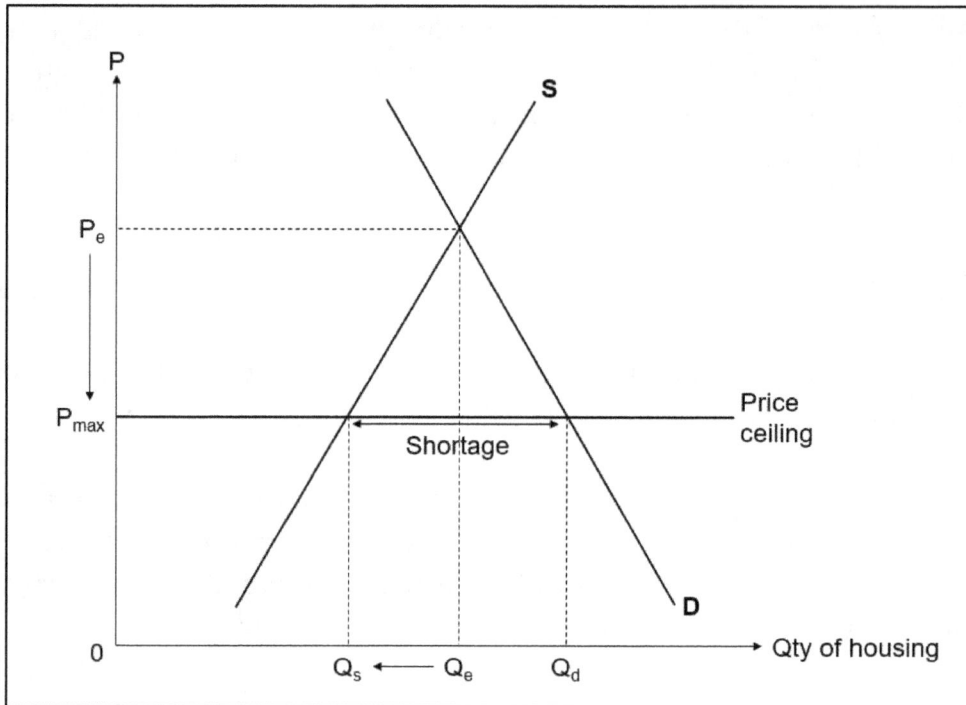

Fig. 15. Consequences of a Price Ceiling in the Housing Market.

5. However, such a scheme could result in housing units of poor quality, since the government lacks the profit motive that private producers have. It could also severely strain the government's budget and incur high opportunity cost as above-mentioned. This may be exacerbated by the inefficiencies that often plague direct provisions due to the lack of profit motive and thus a lack of cost consciousness.

Conclusion

1. The government should only intervene in the housing market when it deems that there is significant enough reason to do so — for instance, due to soaring housing prices or a severe market failure as previously discussed.

2. In other scenarios, government intervention is likely to do more harm than good.

10. Discuss the view that the overuse of common access resources is best addressed by the government. (15)

Introduction

1. Common access resources refer to gifts of nature which are non-excludable but rivalrous in nature.

2. Non-excludable means that it is impossible, or highly difficult, to prevent any one person from consuming the good once it is provided. Rivalrous means that one person's consumption of the good reduces the quantity/quality of said good available for others.

Explanation of Common Access Resources

1. Fundamentally, the free market and the price mechanism exist to maximise the benefit gained by consumers and producers. In the lack of externalities, free market forces are preferred, as they will maximise consumer and producer surplus, and maximise efficiency. However, the free market fails to take into account externalities.

2. One example of a common access resource is the fish in the oceans.

3. Since common access resources are non-excludable, there is nothing preventing people from over-fishing and exploiting the fish population for their own personal gain. Since fishes are available to all and at no cost, consumers and producers in the free market would seek to maximise the amount of fish caught and consumed.

4. As a result, the price mechanism fails to function with a common access resource, and consumers over-consume the resource, generating negative externalities. Negative externalities refer to spill-over costs generated from an activity that impact third-parties, other than the producer or consumer.

5. In this case, the spill-over cost is the threat to sustainability arising from over-fishing – namely, the depletion of fish stock at rate faster than the fishes themselves can reproduce – and the third party in question is future generations who have less fish available for their consumption.

6. Therefore, at each and every quantity Q there is a Marginal External Cost (MEC) resulting from this spillover effect that is not taken into account by the free market. This causes a divergence between the Marginal Private Cost (MPC) and the Marginal Social Cost (MSC) curves, where MSC > MPC, the difference of which is the MEC.

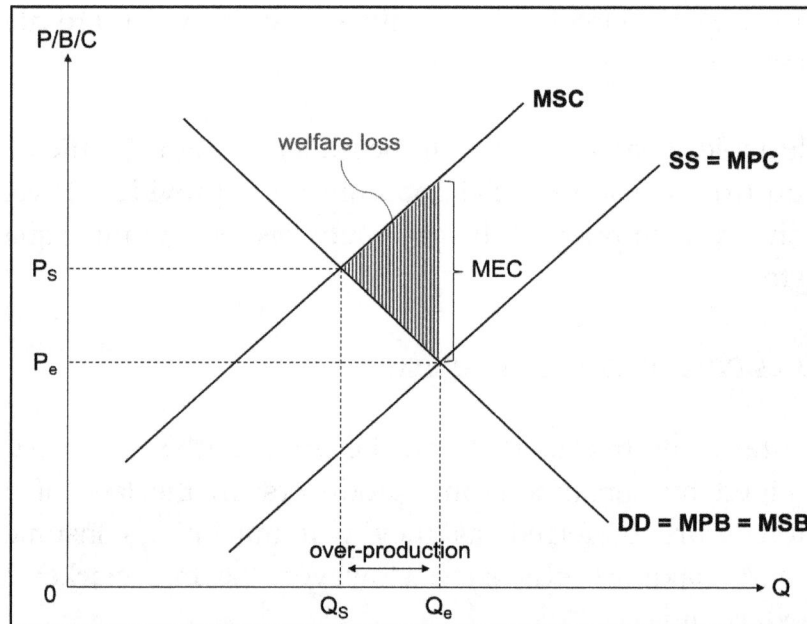

Fig. 16. Overuse of Common Access Resources leading to Market Failure.

7. At the free market amount of consumption, Qe, MSC > MPC, which implies that the last unit of fishing incurs more costs to society than additional benefits. Hence, reducing fishing to levels below Qe would increase societal welfare.

8. The socially-optimal amount is Qs, where MSC equals MSB. Thus, over-fishing represented by Qs – Qe in the Fig. 16 above.

9. For the units Qs – Qe, total social costs are greater than total social benefits. Allocative inefficiency occurs, hence leading to market failure and a deadweight welfare loss (as shaded in diagram) incurred.

10. Hence, if left up to the free market, over-fishing would result, and this poses a severe threat to sustainability, which refers to the ability to fulfil present needs without compromising on the ability to meet the needs of future generations.

11. Consequently, it is up to the government to address the overuse of common access resources, as the free market has failed to do so. It is the government's role to maximise societal well-being, and to ensure that the interests of all in society are taken care of.

Thesis 1: Government policies to address overuse

1. There are several policies the government can adopt to best address the overuse of common access resources.

2. One such policy involves legislation – the government can pass laws that restrict people's ability to exploit and degrade common access resources. For example, in Germany the government holds all vehicles to the Euro emissions standard, requiring that they must have a catalytic converter installed, to reduce the emission of toxic pollutants. These pollutants would otherwise have degraded the quality of the atmosphere, presenting a threat to sustainability. (In this case, clean air is the common access resource that was being exploited.)

3. An alternative policy would be to allocate property rights to individuals. For example, in Indonesia, the Ministry of Marine Affairs and Fisheries has set up managed-access fishing areas, which allocates fishermen a designated area within which to fish. By allocating property rights, this incentivises fishermen to take the initiative to not overfish, with the intention of preventing their allocated property from facing depletion of fish stock.

4. Governments can also intervene through the implementation of carbon taxes. A carbon tax refers to a levy or fee that companies need to pay for the emission of carbon. For example, Singapore is looking to implement a carbon tax from 2020 onwards, wherein facilities producing more than 25,000 tonnes of greenhouse gas emissions will be taxed at $5 per tonne of greenhouse gases. This carbon tax forces polluters to internalise the negative externalities, providing them with a market-based incentive to reduce their pollution down to socially-optimal levels, preventing the exploitation of clean air, a common access resource.

5. Alternatively, governments can implement a tradable pollution permit system as a way to limit the carbon emissions. Each company is allocated a permit to emit a given amount of pollutants over a given time period. These permits are traded freely on the free market. A company that emits more pollutants will have to purchase permits from other companies' excess permits. However, only a fixed number of permits are allocated by the government, effectively creating a 'cap' on the total amount of pollutants that can be emitted. Similarly, the exploitation of clean air is prevented.

Anti-Thesis 1: Government Policies are ineffective

1. However, government policies can be ineffective in dealing with the overuse of common access resources.

2. For legislation, much depends on the strength of the institutional factors at work. Germany, with a strong legal framework and adequate monitoring capabilities, ensures that vehicles must undergo and pass a pollution test every two years, and cars which fail the test must be repaired. In other countries with poor institutional factors, legislation would be ineffective as offenders cannot be easily caught or prosecuted. However, in Indonesia, a lack of strict monitoring and enforcement, as well as widespread institutional corruption, has caused the allocation of property rights to be weak and meaningless.

3. As for carbon taxes, government intervention is likely to exacerbate the situation instead. Governments are unable to accurately determine the 'correct' level of taxes to be implemented, since any external costs are hard to quantify. If the government over-estimates the cost of pollution, it might have taxed too much and cause an under-production instead. In this case, there might even be a larger deadweight welfare loss as compared to before the carbon taxation.

4. Meanwhile, the tradable pollution permits would just lead to other sources of market failure arising. For instance, large firms could begin buying the permits from other firms and hoarding them, hence forcing smaller firms to leave the market. With smaller firms exiting, the large firms hence gain market dominance and cause problems with allocative inefficiency.

Anti-Thesis 2: Best addressed through International Agreements

1. In lieu of governmental action, international agreements are a compelling alternative to address the overuse of common access resources.

2. For example, since many whale species were being hunted to extinction in the 20th Century, there are now international agreements in place that outlaw the hunting of whales, enacted in 1986 by the International Whaling Commission (IWC). These agreements work on the principle that all governments involved agree to the rules established.

3. However, these agreements are fundamentally non-binding; they depend on each country's willingness to adhere to the guidelines stipulated. One notable case-in-point is the Japanese government's recent announcement that it will exit from the IWC in order to resume commercial whaling activities.

4. Nonetheless, there are instances where such international agreements are able to achieve significant progress. For example, the 1987 Montreal Protocol called for a ban on Chlorofluorocarbons (CFCs), greenhouse gases which are especially detrimental to the ozone layer. This agreement was intended to prevent the overuse and degradation of the ozone layer, and it has succeeded in bringing CFC emissions near to zero. This illustrates that international agreements can prove to be effective if all countries are on board.

Conclusion/Synthesis

1. If left to the free market, common access resources will always be overused, generating negative externalities in the process and presenting a threat to sustainability.

2. Since the overuse of common access resources is a global issue, leaving individual governments to tackle the issue on their own might be counter-productive.

3. Much benefits would need to be achieved through international agreements, which serve to unify the approach of world governments and codify their resolve to eradicate the problem.

4. However, just as there is no one-size-fits-all solution, an international agreement could not possibly allow for policy approaches that are tailored to the unique circumstances of each country. It is up to the government to ensure that policies enacted are best suited to handle the overuse within the financial, geopolitical and sociocultural context of each country.

5. Hence, governmental action, in tandem with international agreements, would be the best way to address the overuse of common access resources.

11. Discuss the view that governments should tax the consumption of gasoline (petroleum). (15)

Introduction

1. An indirect tax refers to a levy or fee that has to be paid to the government but the burden of it can be shifted to another party. Tax on gasoline is an example.

Thesis 1: Over-consumption of gasoline

1. The consumption of gasoline is said to generate negative externalities. Negative externalities are costs inflicted on third parties, other than the consumers or producers of gasoline, and for which no compensation is provided.

2. In this case, the external costs include air pollution from the combustion of gasoline, which releases toxic pollutants that leads to health problems like lung cancer. This affects residents, especially those who live near motorways.

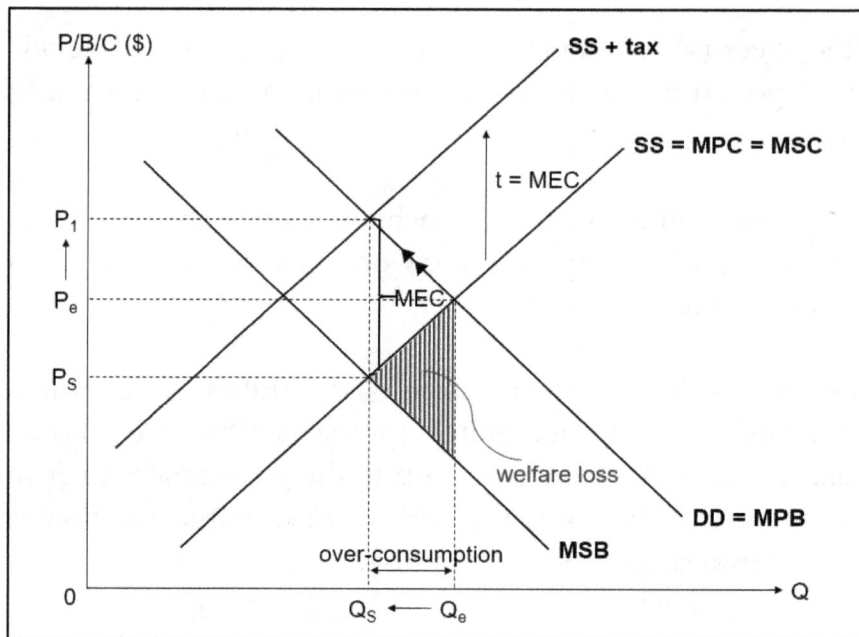

Fig. 17. Over-Consumption of Gasoline leading to Market Failure.

3. Consumers would only consider the personal benefit to them when they consume gasoline. Consequently, the free market transacts at Qe, where the Marginal Private Benefit (MPB) = Demand (DD) curve meets the Marginal Private Cost (MPC) = Supply (SS) curve.

35

4. However, at each and every quantity Q there is a Marginal External Cost (MEC) generated resulting from this spillover effect. This causes a divergence between the MPB and the Marginal Social Benefit (MSB) curves, where MPB > MSB, the difference of which is the MEC. The socially-optimal output is Qs, where MSB equals Marginal Social Cost (MSC). This means that the last unit of gasoline consumed incurs a cost to society that is equivalent to the benefit derived by society from consuming it.

5. At the transacted quantity Qe, MSC > MSB, and there is an over-consumption of gasoline represented by Qe – Qse in Fig. 17 on the previous page. There is over-allocation of scarce resources to the production of gasoline and thus the free market fails to achieve allocative efficiency.

6. A welfare loss to society is incurred since total social costs for the units over-consumed are greater than total social benefits. The welfare loss area corresponds to the shaded region on Fig. 17.

7. Consequently, governments might intervene to resolve this market failure by imposing an indirect tax on gasoline. The imposition of the tax leads to an increase in the marginal cost of production, reducing their profit margins, hence disincentivising them from producing. This causes supply to decrease from SS to SS + tax.

8. The decrease in supply creates a shortage at the original equilibrium price Pe, causing prices to be bidded up to P_1. As a result, the quantity of gasoline transacted decreases from Qe to Qs, the socially optimal level.

9. This would serve to eliminate the welfare loss to society, thereby correcting the market failure.

10. The same argument can also be applied to the problem of congestion, another example of negative externality, caused by private transport. Taxing gasoline would raise the Marginal Private Costs of using Private Transport, thereby alleviating the over-consumption.

Thesis 2: Tax revenue

1. Additionally, a tax levied on gasoline has the potential to be a big source of revenue for the government. This is fundamentally due to the nature of gasoline as a widely-used commodity and with a lack of substitutes.

2. Diagrammatically, the revenue accrued through an excise tax on gasoline is represented by ($t x Qs) in Fig. 17.

3. For example, the United States has a federal tax on gasoline at a rate of 18.4 cents per gallon. In the Fiscal Year 2014, this tax was responsible for generating US$ 25 billion in revenue for the federal government.

4. This is a significant sum of money which the government could devote towards a variety of projects. In the case of the United States, the bulk of this revenue goes towards funding infrastructure projects such as the construction of highways, while the remainder is used to alleviate the fiscal constraints experienced by the government.

Anti-Thesis 1: Ineffective at reducing consumption

1. If the government's primary motive is in implementing the tax is to discourage the consumption of gasoline, there might be better alternative policies to achieve the same effect.

2. For one, since the demand for gasoline tends to be price inelastic due to a lack of substitutes available, the quantity transacted of gasoline would decrease less-than-proportionately as compared to increase in price arising from the tax. Therefore, it could take an extremely high tax per unit in order to reduce quantity consumed to the socially-optimal level.

3. This may not be acceptable to the citizens and may thus prove to be a rather politically infeasible policy to implement effectively. For example, in 2017 the French government attempted to increase the tax on gasoline as a measure to combat global warming and climate change. This was deeply unpopular, and lead to weeks of continuous riots and protests involving at least 280,000 protesters across France.

4. A better policy to reduce congestion could be to expand and improve the private transportation system to make it more convenient, comfortable and faster. That way, commuters will on their own accord switch away from using private transport.

5. To tackle pollution caused by the use of gasoline, legislation mandating the use of certain filters to remove pollutants emitted could be implemented. This could incur fewer costs to consumers, and would thus be more acceptable to the populace.

Anti-Thesis 2: Measurement difficulties

1. The correct amount of tax per unit should be equivalent to the MEC. However, it is extremely difficult to attach a monetary valuation to the externality generated.

2. Thus, any tax imposed may not significantly correct the market failure and if over-taxation occurs, under-consumption and a larger deadweight welfare loss may occur, resulting in Government failure.

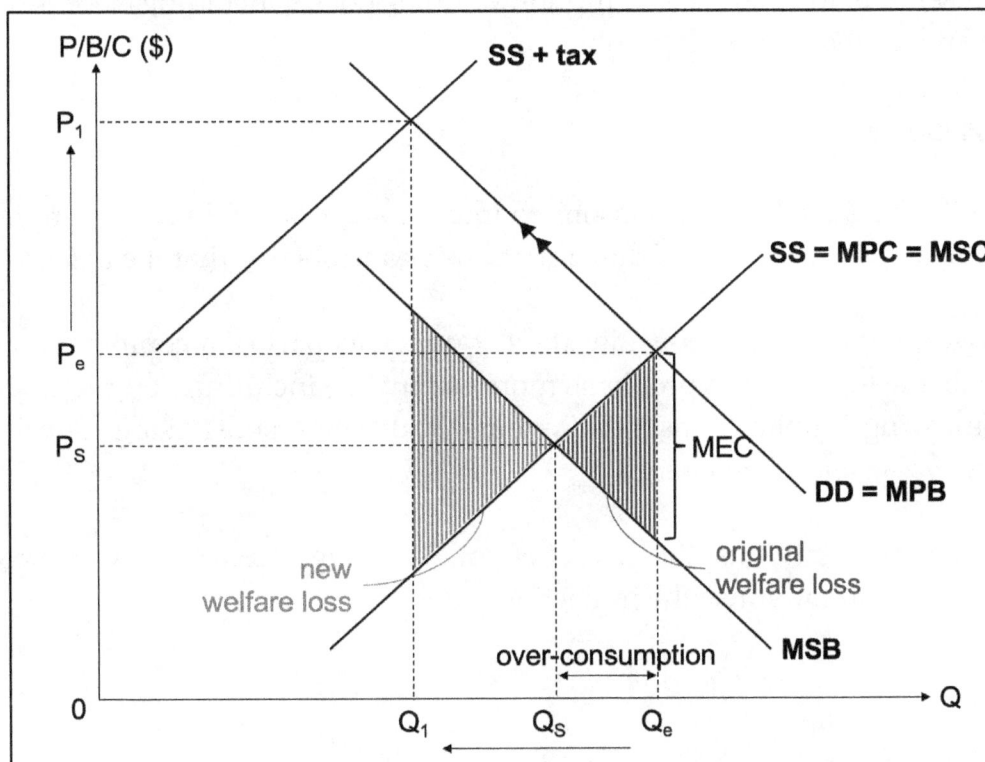

Fig. 18. Over-tax leading to an Increased Welfare Loss.

3. Referring to Fig. 18 above, if the government were to over-tax, the quantity of gasoline consumed would fall so significantly (below Q_S) to Q_1, causing an even larger deadweight welfare loss to be incurred.

4. Hence, due to information failure, government intervention has caused larger allocative inefficiency in this case.

Anti-Thesis 3: Inequity

1. Furthermore, a tax on gasoline would disproportionately impact the poor. Being an indirect tax, it is regressive in nature, which means that it will take up a larger proportion of the income of the low-income earner compared to the high-income earner.

2. This problem is especially acute if public transport systems are under-developed, and cars constitute the primary means by which people, even the poor, commute to school/work. In this case, the gasoline tax would directly affect the prices that these low-income earners will have to pay for transportation.

3. Higher prices of gasoline may also contribute to increased public transport fares.

4. Thus, a tax on gasoline may be considered inequitable, forcing the low-income households to forego consumption of other goods including necessities in order to finance the increased gasoline prices.

Conclusion

1. While there are be valid reasons to impose a tax on gasoline, its implementation must take into account of the limitations and problems that it can lead to.

2. Governments should consider the tax policy as part of a combination of policies available to tackle the problems more effectively, including long term policies like improving public transport systems and even subsidising development of renewable and clean energy.

3. Where necessary, gasoline tax relief vouchers targeted at the lower income can be rolled out to minimise the impact on them.

12. Explain why when producer and consumer surplus is maximised, allocative efficiency is achieved. (10)

<u>Introduction</u>

1. Allocative efficiency refers to the scenario where scarce resources are distributed between competing needs in the best possible manner. This means that the 'right' amount of resources are being allocated to the production of a specific good.

2. Consumer surplus is defined as the highest price consumers are willing to pay for a good minus the price actually paid.

3. Producer surplus is defined as the price received by firms for selling their good minus the lowest price that they are willing to accept to produce the good.

<u>Diagram and elaboration</u>

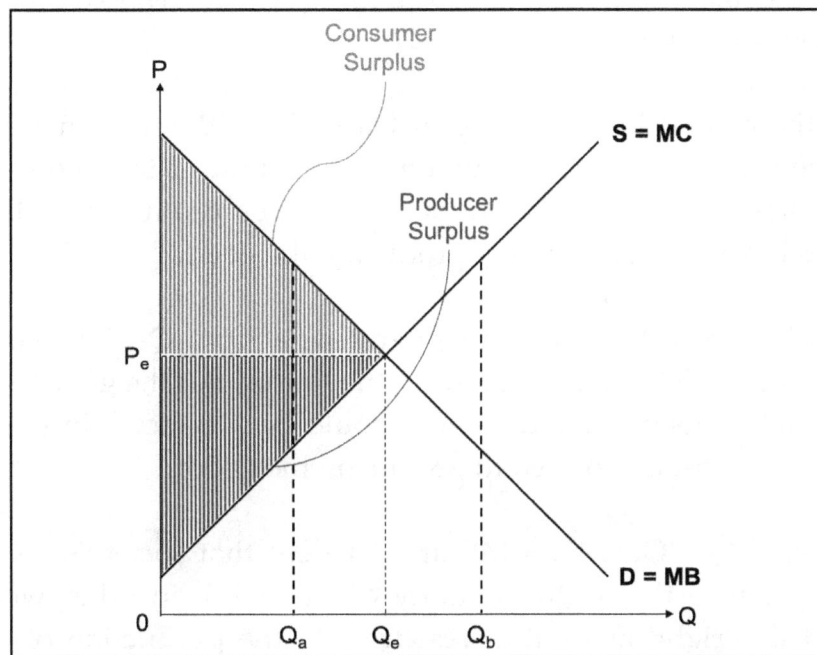

Fig. 19. Consumer and Producer Surplus, illustrated.

1. Market equilibrium occurs at the point of intersection of the demand and supply curves, at Qe units produced. At the point of competitive market equilibrium, the sum of consumer and producer surplus is maximum.

2. To see why, consider what would happen if any quantity less than Qe were produced. If, say, Qa is produced, the sum of consumer plus producer surplus would be smaller, as this sum would be equal to the shaded area between the demand and supply curves only up to output Qa. It follows, then, that the sum of consumer plus producer surplus is maximised at the point of market equilibrium.

3. If we interpret the demand curve as a marginal benefit (MB) curve, and the supply curve as a marginal cost (MC) curve, then market equilibrium occurs where MB = MC.

4. Marginal Benefit refers to the benefit to society derived from consuming an additional unit of the good. Marginal Cost refers to the cost to society arising from the production of an additional unit of the good.

5. The equality of MB with MC tells us that, at Qe, the extra benefit to society of getting one more unit of the good is equal to the extra cost to society of producing one more unit of the good.

6. Should the market be producing at Qa < Qe, MB > MC, meaning that society would be placing a greater value on the last unit of the good produced than it costs to produce it, and so more of it should be produced. In this case, too few resources have been allocated to producing the good.

7. Conversely, should the market be producing at Qb > Qe, MC > MB, meaning that it would cost society more to produce the last unit of the good produced than the value society puts on it, and so less should be produced. In this case, too many resources have been allocated to producing the good.

8. Therefore, at Q = Qe, MC = MB, it is evident that society's resources are being used to produce the 'right' quantity of the good; in other words, society has allocated the 'right' amount of resources to the production of the good, and is producing the quantity of the good that is mostly wanted by society..

Conclusion

1. Therefore, it is evident that allocative efficiency is achieved when consumer and producer surplus are maximised.

2. However, it is worthy to note that efficiency can only arise under a number of very strict and highly unrealistic conditions that are practically never met in the real world. In the real world the market fails with respect to achieving both allocative and productive efficiency. Market failures are an important justification for government intervention.

13. Discuss the view that we should rely solely on market-based measures to tackle carbon emissions. (15)

<u>Introduction</u>

1. Carbon emission refers to the total amount of greenhouse gases produced from human activities. Such emissions are generated from the consumption and production of goods and services, hence it is a case of negative externalities.

2. Negative externalities refer to an adverse impact, arising from consumption or production activities, on third-parties not involved in the economic transaction.

3. As such, the government is incentivised to intervene, alleviating the negative externality so as to prevent market failure.

4. Market-based measures include a carbon tax, and a system of tradable pollution permits. Non-market based measures include regulations and education.

<u>Explanation of carbon tax</u>

1. A tax on emissions refers to a levy or fee that electricity companies need to pay for the emission of various polluting gases, that are typically by-products of the burning of fossil fuels and other industrial processes.

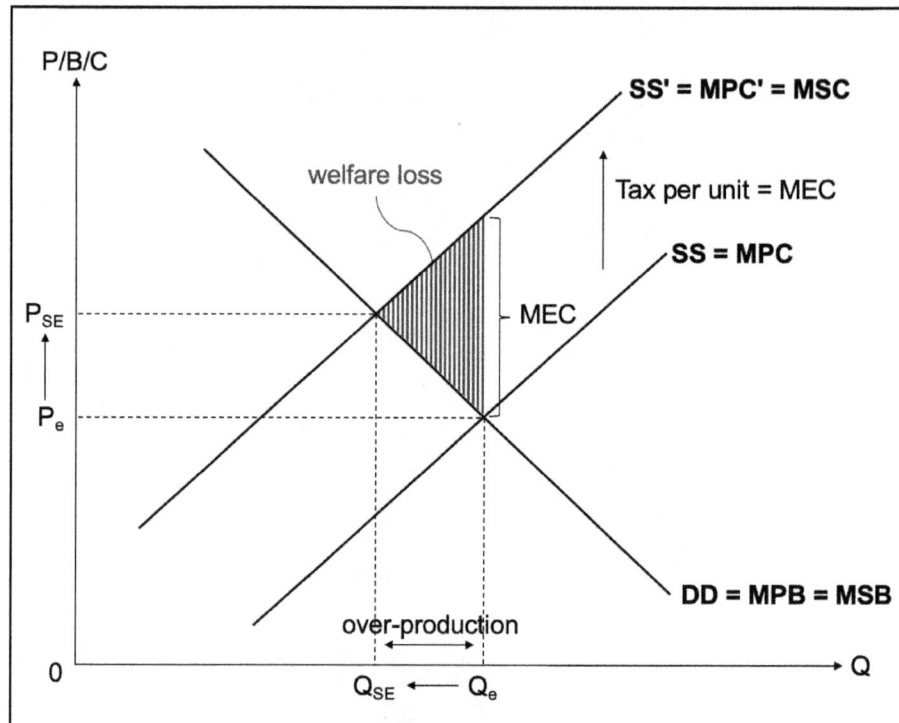

Fig. 20. Carbon Tax to reduce Emissions.

2. For example, Singapore is looking to implement a carbon tax from 2020 onwards, wherein facilities producing more than 25,000 tonnes of greenhouse gas emissions will be taxed at $5 per tonne of greenhouse gases.

3. The tax effectively raises the cost of production for firms. The carbon tax will raise the producers' marginal private costs of production (MPC), diagrammatically represented as an upward shift of MPC to MPC'. Assuming the tax per unit is equal to MEC, the MPC curve shifts upwards by the amount of MEC. With the carbon tax, the new market equilibrium output, where MPB = MPC', will coincide at the socially-optimal output level where MSB = MSC. Production falls from Qe to the socially-optimal level Qse, eliminating the welfare loss indicated by the shaded area in Fig. 20, and allowing allocative efficiency to be achieved.

Evaluation of carbon tax

1. The tax revenue collected could then be channelled to fund research schemes into methods to reduce carbon emissions. For instance, research into alternative energy sources like solar power, which generate significantly less carbon emissions than fossil fuel. This could provide a long-term solution to the problem of carbon emissions.

2. This tax on emissions forces polluters to internalise the external costs of pollution, incentivising them to develop technologies to reduce the level of greenhouse gas emissions. Companies might seek to use carbon-scrubbing technology to decrease the amount of greenhouse gases emitted. Otherwise, they may adopt 'green' production techniques which are less polluting.

3. However, in reality, there are data constraints caused by imperfect information. The government is unlikely to have perfectly accurate information on the level of MEC at the socially-optimal output. This is due to the inherent difficulties in quantifying the precise level of external costs that third parties bear. Some of these costs could be very abstract and difficult to put into numbers, for instance the detriment on future generations as a result of global warming caused by carbon emissions. Thus it is very difficult for the government to estimate the exact magnitude of tax that is required.

4. Furthermore, firms in specific industries are also likely to pass on the burden of the tax to consumers. For instance, the demand for electricity is highly price inelastic, as it is a necessity good required in almost all aspects of daily life. Thus, electricity producers are likely to pass on the costs of the carbon tax on to consumers in the form of increased prices; this could have severe repercussions on lower-income households, who may not be able to afford the increased prices. Additionally, the firms themselves, bearing little of the tax burden, are less incentivised to cut back on pollution, rendering the carbon tax relatively ineffective at tackling their carbon emissions.

Explanation of tradable pollution permits

1. A tradable pollution permit system is a way to limit the amount of pollutants emitted. The government first decides on an optimal level of carbon emissions that is allowable. It then creates permits, which allow companies to emit a certain amount of carbon over a given period. These permits are then allocated to companies, serving as an effective 'limit' on the amount each company can emit. Companies that go beyond the limit will have to purchase permits from other companies who have excess. Companies that are under the limit can profit from selling their excess permits. This incentivises companies to reduce the amount of carbon emissions.

2. For example, Sweden implemented its Emissions Trading Scheme (ETS) in 2005. Swedish companies must have a special permit to emit carbon dioxide from 2005, without which no emission allowances will be allocated.

Evaluation of tradable pollution permits

1. A scheme of tradable pollution permits incentivises firms to reduce their carbon emissions by adopting more eco-friendly methods of production. This is effective at addressing the root of the issue.

2. Firms would also seek to lower carbon emissions in the least costly manner in order to maximise profitability, leading to lower emission levels compared to non market-based measures like legislation.

3. However, such policies are administratively complex. It is extremely difficult to determine the 'correct' level of pollution, since external costs (especially those on future generations) are hard to quantify.

4. Additionally, in real life the system has been ineffective due to a huge surplus of allowances (pollution permits). Practically speaking, this means almost all companies are allocated more permits than they can use. Obviously, this would do little to encourage companies to cut back on pollution.

Explanation of non market-based measures

1. One such measure involves the use of legislation. The government could influence firms' behaviour by imposing regulations, compelling firms to take certain actions to reduce their carbon emissions. For instance, the government could set a limit on the amount of emissions a factory is allowed to produce, or it could direct firms to use technologies like carbon-scrubbing to reduce their emissions.

2. Another such measure involves the use of education campaigns, wherein the government educates consumers on the impact of carbon emissions on them and future generations. Consumers are educated on which firms are ecologically-friendly, in hopes that they will support firms which adopt environmental practices.

Evaluation of non market-based measures

1. Legislative measures are easy to implement, compared with tradable pollution permits. It also has a very clear and definite effect compared with carbon tax; the government need not attempt to anticipate how markets would react to the imposition of a tax.

2. However, legislation creates no market-based incentives for firms to reduce emissions beyond what is legally stipulated. This measure does not differentiate whether firms face high or low costs when forced to reduce pollution, therefore pollution is lowered at a higher overall cost compared to market-based measures.

3. Additionally, the effectiveness of legislation overwhelmingly hinges upon the strength of the institutional factors concerned. Close monitoring needs to be enacted to ensure companies are abiding by the law, enforcement measures need to be put in place to ensure compliance, and there needs to be stringent penalties for flouting the legislative measures. If any one of these three factors is missing, companies will see little need to abide by the legislation, rendering it ineffective at countering carbon emissions.

4. Education campaigns could be a good long-term solution in changing the mindset of consumers, encouraging them to be more involved in environmental causes, and to engage in conscious consumption.

5. However, such education campaigns have uncertain effectiveness. Many consumers are apathetic towards environmental damage, making them resistant to such educational messaging. Consumers may also be unwilling to bear the increased prices that come with supporting 'green' firms. Impacts of such educational campaigns will also take a long time to materialise, and the impact of such policies, if any, will not be evident for a long time.

Conclusion/Synthesis

1. Market-based measures are not the be-all-and-end-all to reducing carbon emissions.

2. Different approaches should be used for different industries. For certain industries, existing technologies can already reduce emissions at low cost. In such cases, it would be more effective to mandate the adoption of such technology.

3. The severity of the problem should also be considered. For example, in China, where carbon emissions are skyrocketing, the problem is so severe that simply restricting production via legislation would be more effective than market-based measures.

4. Ultimately, to alleviate the global warming threat arising from human activities, looking at carbon emissions alone is drastically insufficient. There are other, far more potent greenhouse gases, whose emissions should be an equal cause for concern. Focussing only on carbon emissions and neglecting those of other greenhouse gases would be a major oversight.

14. Explain what is involved in rational decision making by both consumers and producers. (10)

Introduction

1. Economies face the problem of scarcity: unlimited wants but limited resources

2. Consequently, decisions have to be made to allocate resources.

3. Such decisions will incur opportunity costs: the next best alternative forgone.

4. The rational decision making process is often based on the marginalist principle. Decision makers compare the marginal benefit against marginal cost of an economic activity.

5. Rational consumers will wish to maximise their utility, while rational firms will wish to maximise profits.

Consumers

1. A rational consumer seeks to maximise utility by maximising the net total benefits from consuming a good. This requires the consumer to consider the private marginal benefits against private marginal costs of consuming the good.

2. A rational consumer will buy an extra unit of a good as long as marginal benefit exceeds the price and opportunity cost of purchasing the extra unit of the good.

3. As a consumer consumes a greater quantity of a good, for example bubble tea, the marginal benefit derived from drinking each cup (such as enjoyment and quenching one's thirst) falls. This is due to the law of diminishing marginal returns. Thus, the price the consumer is willing to pay for more units of bubble tea also falls.

4. This is shown in the downward sloping demand curve as seen below in Fig. 21.

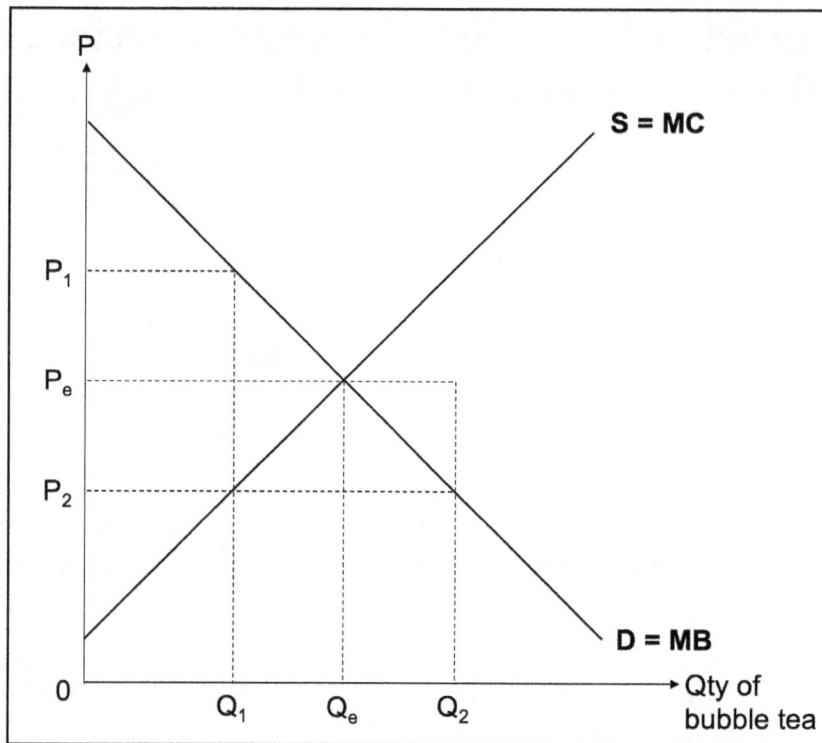

Fig. 21. Market for Bubble Tea.

5. In consuming Q1 unit of output, the consumer incurs opportunity cost which is the benefits derived from the next best alternative forgone. This is measured as the price of the good, at Pe in the Fig. 21.

6. Rational consumers will buy a particular unit if the marginal benefits outweigh the marginal costs. At Q_1, since $0P_1$ is more than OPe, consumers will buy this unit.

7. Consumers will buy up to the point Qe since for all units before Qe, the additional benefits are higher than the additional costs.

8. It is irrational to consume any units beyond Qe as the marginal costs are higher than the marginal benefits. For example, for Q_2 unit of consumption, the opportunity cost $0Pe$ is higher than the benefit $0P_2$, it is better for the consumer to forgo this unit of bubble tea.

Producers

1. A rational firm seeks to maximise total profits from the production and sale of a good.

2. Rational decision making by firms means that firms will base their output decision on the marginal revenue (the price the good is sold at) and marginal cost of producing the good.

3. A rational firm will want to profit maximise, and produce and sell an additional unit of a good, like a cup of bubble tea, for example, as long as the MR is larger than MC.

4. With reference to Fig. 21, at Q_1 unit of output, the private benefit of the producers is seen at price Pe.

5. The marginal costs for the producer, that includes the additional costs of starch pearls, tea leaves and labour used in producing the extra cup, increases with a higher quantity of bubble tea produced. This is seen in the upward sloping supply curve.

6. It shows the minimum price that producers are willing and able to sell their goods for and it is also the benefits (payment) they will get if they use the resources to produce another good.

7. With reference to Fig. 21, for Q_1 unit of output, the opportunity cost to producers is P_2.

8. Rational producers will produce a particular unit if the marginal benefits outweigh the marginal costs. At Q_1, since 0Pe (market price) is more than $0P_2$, producers will produce this unit.

9. Producers will produce up to the point Qe since for all units before Qe, the additional benefits are higher than the additional costs.

10. It is irrational to produce beyond Qe as the marginal costs are higher than the marginal benefits. For example, at Q_2 unit, the opportunity cost P_1 is higher than the benefit, Pe. It is better for producers to forgo this unit of bubble tea.

Market

1. The marginalist principle is adopted by both consumers and firms when they attempt to maximise their self-interest.

2. The determinants affecting the rational decision making is thus the marginal benefits and marginal costs of the consumer and producer.

3. When resource allocation is left to the price mechanism, goods are produced up to a point where demand matches supply. Since demand reflects MB and supply reflects MC, at the market equilibrium point where demand meets supply, MB = MC. The market equilibrium price of Pe is also the prevailing price Pe, which is the MC of consumers, and MB of firms.

15. Recently, Switzerland held a national referendum to decide on whether to implement a minimum wage. Discuss how you would have voted if such a referendum was held in your country. (15)

<u>Introduction</u>

1. A minimum wage is a price floor for wages where the objective is usually to raise the income of poorer, low-skilled workers such that there will be less income inequality in the country and to improve equity.

<u>Explanation of minimum wage</u>

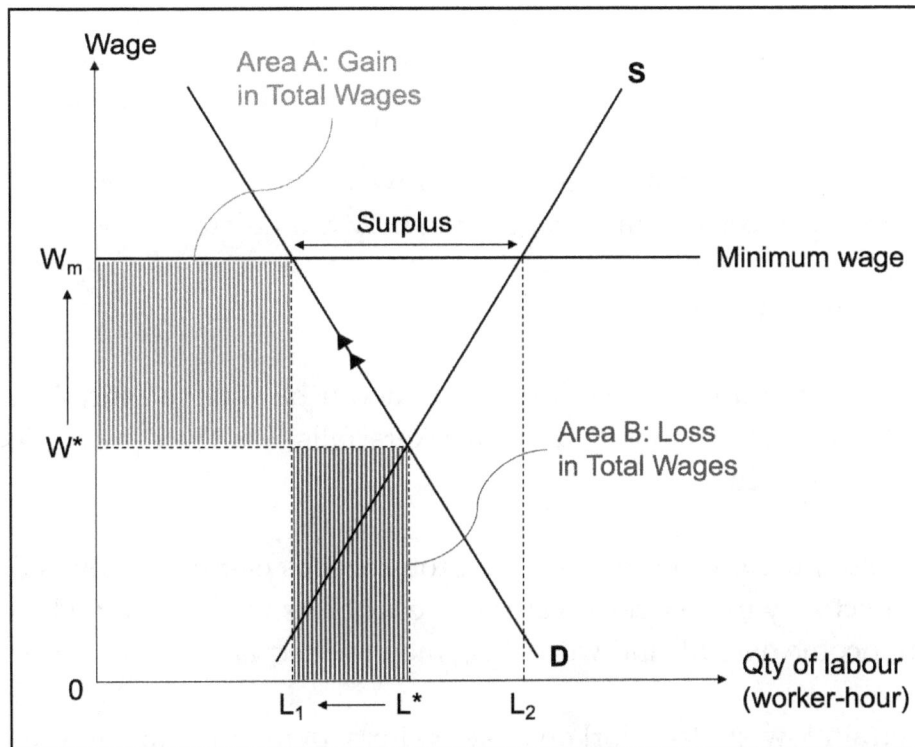

Fig. 22. Effects of Minimum Wage on Total Wages.

1. Originally, employment is at L^* and the equilibrium wage is W^*, derived from the intersection of the Demand (D) and Supply (S) curves for labour.

2. After a minimum wage of Wm is implemented above the equilibrium wage W^*, the quantity of labour demanded falls from L^* to L_1, and the quantity of labour supplied increases from L^* to L_2. A surplus of $L_2 - L_1$ is created.

3. In Fig. 22, Area A represents the increase in total wages earned by low-skilled workers as a result of the minimum wage, while Area B represents the decrease in total wages due to retrenchment.

Pros of minimum wage

1. By setting the minimum wage, the income of these low-skilled workers is raised. This improves their standard of living, allowing them to afford more goods and services.

2. Assuming the demand for such labour is wage inelastic, Area A > Area B, and the total income accrued by low-skilled workers increases, since the quantity demanded for workers falls less than proportionately to the increase in wages.

3. For certain low-skilled workers, like garbage collectors, demand is likely to be wage-inelastic as it is still too difficult to replace them with machines.

4. This allows income distribution to improve on a whole, as low-skilled workers as a whole now receive higher wages than they did before.

Cons of minimum wage

1. However, should the demand for such labour be wage elastic, Area B > Area A, since the quantity demanded for workers falls less than proportionately to the increase in wages.

2. As a result, there is a net loss of the total wages earned by low-skilled workers. This effectively makes the lower-income workers worse off than before, earning a lower income overall, and worsening income inequality.

3. For certain low-skilled workers, like waiters, demand is likely to be wage-elastic as it is increasingly feasible to replace them with self ordering and paying machines as well as drones and conveyor belts for serving.

4. Regardless of the wage elasticity of demand, the policy will always result in some amount of unemployment. The decrease in the quantity demanded of labour from L^* to L_1 represents the retrenchments that occur as a result of the policy. Workers who are retrenched are obviously worse off than before.

5. Another concern is that a black market for labour could arise, wherein workers are employed at a wage lower than what is legally required. Often, these workers are undocumented, and thus receive little protection in terms of safety, healthcare, and overtime pay. Therefore, in addition to reduced pay, these workers also face threats to their standard of living, as their health and safety may be put at risk in the workplace.

6. There is also a deadweight loss to society associated with the minimum wage, arising since scarce labour resources are no longer optimally utilised once the policy goes into effect. There is now an under-utilisation of low-skilled workers compared to the socially optimal amount at Q^*.

7. In addition, for a small and open economy like Singapore where exports and foreign direct investments are critical for economic growth, there is a need to maintain cost-competitiveness. A minimum wage would raise unit labour costs, reducing the Short-run Aggregate Supply of the economy, reducing economic growth and increasing demand-deficient unemployment. It is thus also undesirable from a macroeconomic point of view.

Alternative policy: increasing productivity of low-skilled workers

1. Low-skilled workers could be trained to become more productive. For example, policies could target training workers to become more familiar with automated production techniques. This policy is widely-used in Singapore. For example, equipping cleaners with the know-how to operate machines allow them to clean more floors per day — enabling technology to enhance worker productivity, rather than serving to make workers obsolete. By increasing workers' productivity, the demand for such labour would effectively increase. The increase in demand allows for increased wages.

2. However, compared to a minimum wage policy, steps to raise productivity are likely to be more costly to the government as training subsidies would be required to encourage firms to implement such training and capital investments. There would be little certainty in whether workers would be receptive to such training. There will be long time lags as it takes time to convince the firms and workers as well as for the worker to be trained. In comparison, a minimum wage policy works quickly once enacted.

3. There is also risk of worker-displacement by automation. Unemployment of low-skilled workers who have not improved their skills would likely occur.

Conclusion/Synthesis

1. On balance, from both micro-economic and macro-economic perspectives, I think a minimum wage would not be suitable for Singapore.

2. I would therefore vote against it.

3. Singapore should instead play to its strengths. Its small geographical size and population, relatively literate people as well as its government's large fiscal resources, makes the implementation of training a feasible and effective long-term policy in Singapore.

4. I would vote for the Progressive Wage Model (PWM), which is what the Singapore government has implemented. It is akin to an occupation-specific minimum wage plus training. The PWM specifies the minimum basic wage of say a cleaner with basic certifications, and in addition also spells out how his wages can increase with more years of experiences and additional training. This helps wages to increase beyond the minimum and ensure the increments are in line with productivity growth, thus keeping the economy competitive.

5. In addition, direct subsidies and transfer payments by the Government (funded by progressive income taxes) should still be considered to increase the purchasing power of the low-income households to better ensure their ability to fulfil basic human needs and hence achieve equity.

16. Should Price Discrimination be banned? Discuss. (15)

Introduction

1. Governments are concerned with the microeconomic goals of economic efficiency and equity.

2. As such, the decision to ban price discrimination (PD) or not depends on its effects on the microeconomic goals.

Thesis 1: Should be banned due to Increased Income Inequality and Inequity

1. PD should be banned as it erodes the consumer surplus, which is particularly damaging in the case of 1st degree price discrimination, where the entire consumer surplus (CS) is extracted and transferred from consumer to producers. CS is the difference between the maximum amount that consumers would have been willing and able to pay for the good and what the consumers actually pay.

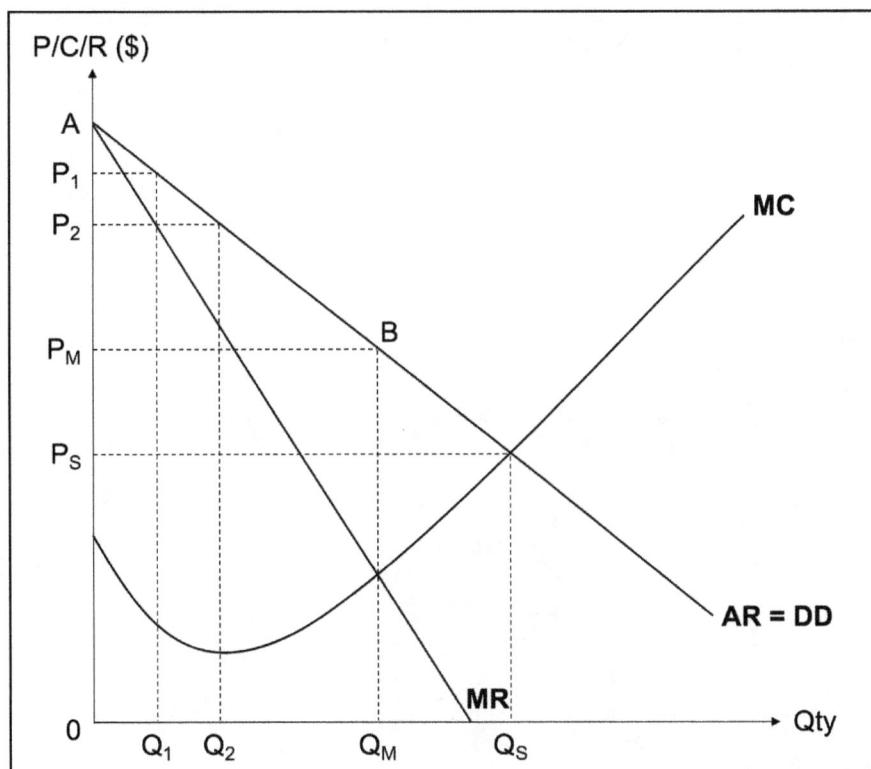

Fig. 23. Loss of Consumer Surplus from 1st Degree Price Discrimination.

2. A non-PD monopolist would have produced at Qm (profit maximising output where Marginal Cost = Marginal Revenue) and charge P_M, as seen in Fig 23. Consumers thus enjoy a surplus of area AP_MB.

3. However, with 1st degree PD, the monopolist will charge the maximum price consumers are willing and able to pay for each individual unit of product. Hence, the first unit Q_1 is charged the price P_1. The second unit Q_2 is charged the price P_2 and so on. Thus, the firm fully absorbs the consumers' surplus, causing CS to fall to zero.

4. The monopolist will also now produce up to Qs, charging a price of Ps for that last unit.

5. The "creaming off" of CS by the firm, allows the firm enjoying more producer surplus, earn higher revenues and greater supernormal profits. This leads to greater concentration of income in the hands of a few, the owners of these firms, which are typically dominant firms, and as such with sufficient market power to price discriminate successfully.

6. This leads to greater income inequality and, along with that, increased inequity as well, since the lower income households will have less income available to afford necessities like food and fulfil basic human needs like healthcare.

7. Such increased inequity is also present in the other types of PD although to a lesser extent, as producers price discriminate with the objective to enjoy higher total revenue and hence higher profits.

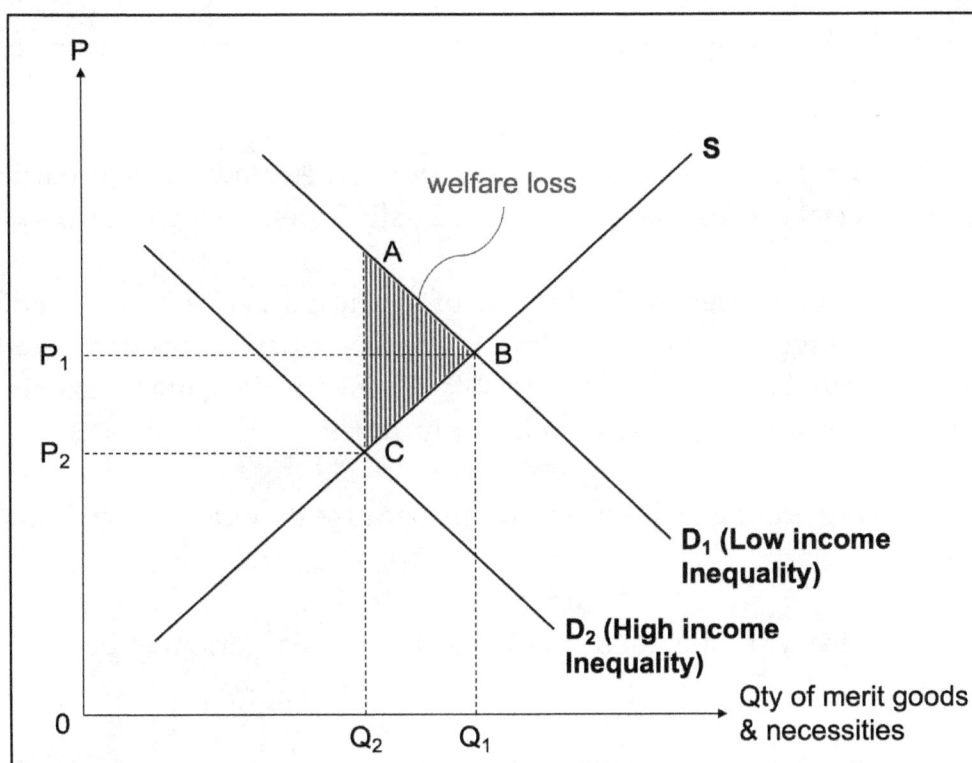

Fig. 24. Under-Consumption due to High degree of Income Inequality.

8. As illustrated in Fig. 24 on the previous page, at D_2, with high income inequality, the masses are lacking in income and therefore lack purchasing power, which in turn affects effective demand due to lack of ability of consumers to pay.

9. This in contrast to effective demand when there is lower degree of income inequality, which will be a higher level of demand D_1 and a more appropriate level of consumption, Q_1.

10. As such, high degree of income inequality leads to under-consumption of necessities and merit goods like healthcare at Q_2.

11. There is thus a deadweight welfare loss of shaded area ABC, arising from inequity.

12. Thus the government should ban PD due to the negative impact of its increasing income inequality and inequity.

Anti-Thesis 1: PD can help achieve equity

1. However, PD can help achieve equity.

2. With price discrimination in place, firms may be willing to provide their goods and services at a lower price to certain groups of consumers because they can charge a higher price for the rest, allowing those low income earners to access the goods.

3. This exists for example in public transport where low income earners may be given a special concession pass with will entitle them to lower prices.

4. This can also be observed in the case of medical services, where patients can be charged a range of prices according to their occupation, residential addresses or income levels because the firm is able to effectively gauge income levels and charge lower prices to those with lower incomes.

5. The firms are willing and able to do this because they can charge higher prices to the rest.

6. Without price discrimination, the lower income earners may be "priced-out" of the market.

7. Thus, PD can help achieve equity and as the consumption of healthcare generates positive externalities, such as reduced susceptibility to illnesses for all, such PD also serves to increase societal welfare.

Anti-Thesis 2: PD can help achieve allocative and dynamic efficiency

1. Monopolies practising 1st degree PD produce at the allocatively-efficient output where $P = MC$ (Marginal Costs)

2. As they can charge different prices at each unit sold, thus the price also becomes equal to the Marginal Revenue.

3. Thus, the profit maximising output will be where the Demand and Marginal Cost curves intersect, which will also be allocatively-efficient as at that output, Qs as seen in Fig. 23, $P = MC$.

4. Furthermore, firms who PD may contribute to an improvement in dynamic efficiency.

5. This is because PD leads to an increase in supernormal profits, which increases their ability to conduct research and development and innovation.

6. Product innovation allows consumers to enjoy more innovative and better quality products, increasing consumer and societal welfare.

7. Process innovation allows the firms to lower their Long Run Average Costs (LRAC), thus achieving greater productive efficiency.

Conclusion/Synthesis

1. On balance, I think PD should not be banned by governments as it is not an altogether harmful practice and can lead to some desirable outcomes through improvements in equity and efficiency.

2. Banning is too extreme a measure.

3. It would be more sensible for the government to consider other policies to mitigate the negative impacts of PD or better manage it to prevent the exploitation of consumers, such as imposing price regulations, price ceilings to limit the differences in prices.

4. The Government's focus should also instead be on reducing market dominance and promoting competition, which should be a better "up-stream" way to keep consumer exploitation in check and also promote efficiency and equity.

17. Discuss how realistic it is to assume that firms want and are able to maximise their profits. (15)

Introduction

1. Profits are defined as the difference between total revenue and total costs, which includes both explicit and implicit costs including opportunity costs, defined as the value of the next best alternative forgone.

Thesis: Realistic & Able to

1. It is realistic for firms to want to maximise profits as they exist to earn profits.

2. This is especially so because a firm's profits has a direct impact on the owner's income. Maximising the firm's profits will generate more income for the owner who can then afford more goods and services and gain more consumer utility.

3. Firms also have the ability to maximise profits, by following the profit maximising condition to produce at a level where marginal costs (MC) = marginal revenue (MR), and where MC is rising.

4. MC is defined as the additional cost of producing one additional unit of output.

5. MR is defined as the additional revenue derived from selling one additional unit of output.

6. At that profit maximising output level, the firm can obtain the profit maximising price from the Demand curve.

7. This is illustrated in Fig. 25 on the next page.

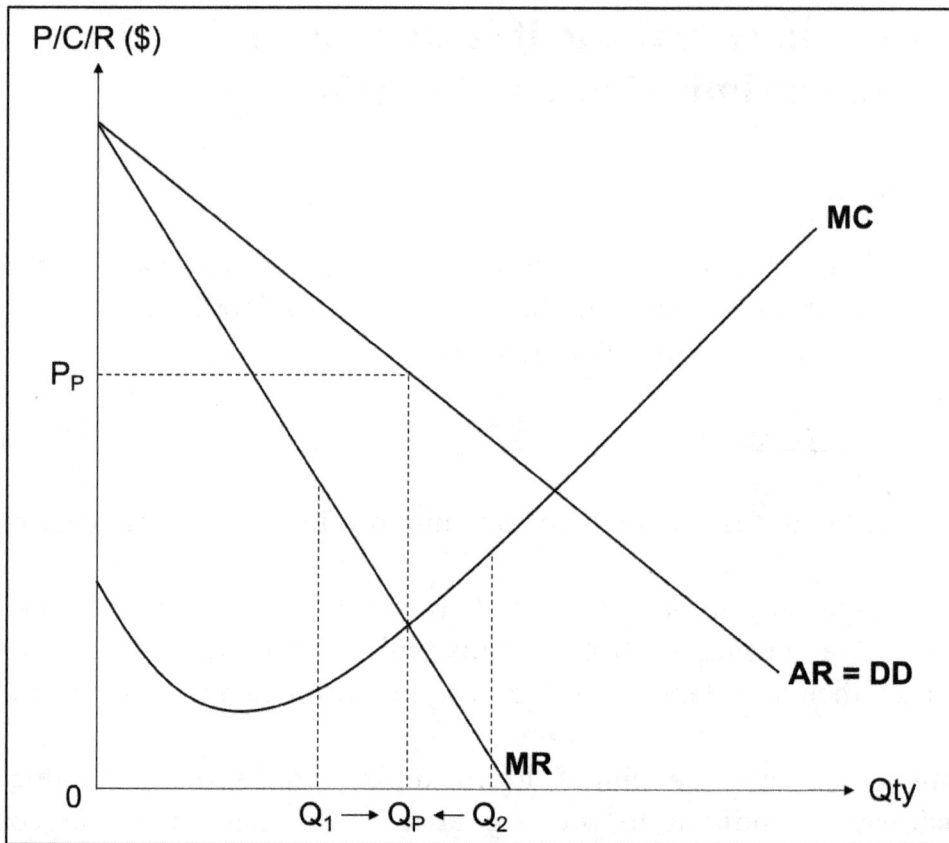

Fig. 25. Profit-Maximising Condition.

8. As seen in Fig. 25, at Q_1, MR exceeds MC. At this point, more profits can still be gained and rational producers will want to increase output towards Q_P where $MC = MR$.

9. On the other hand, at Q_2, MC exceeds MR. At this point, the additional costs incurred from producing the additional unit of good will exceed the additional revenue that can be gained. As such rational producers will wish to reduce output towards Q_P, in order to increase profits.

10. At profit maximising level of output, Q_P, the firm can then derive the appropriate price at P_P from the firm's demand at $DD = AR$.

11. This price and quantity thus allows the firm to be able to attain price maximisation.

Anti-thesis: Not realistic and Unable to

1. However, firms may not be able to maximise their profits as they may lack the necessary information to do so, both in terms of revenue and cost.

2. In reality, firms do not have complete knowledge of their demand, and as such, may not be able to accurately set prices. Exact Marginal Revenues would also be unknown as these are derived from the Average Revenue / Demand curve.

3. Firms also may not be able to take into account all of the costs, especially opportunity cost as the next best alternative forgone may not be accurately known as well as its value.

4. In addition, it may be difficult to derive the additional cost of the "additional" unit, especially when producing and selling at scale.

5. As such, these limitations in terms of information will cause the firm to be unable to determine the profit maximising levels.

6. In addition, there may be government intervention that prevents firms from maximising profits.

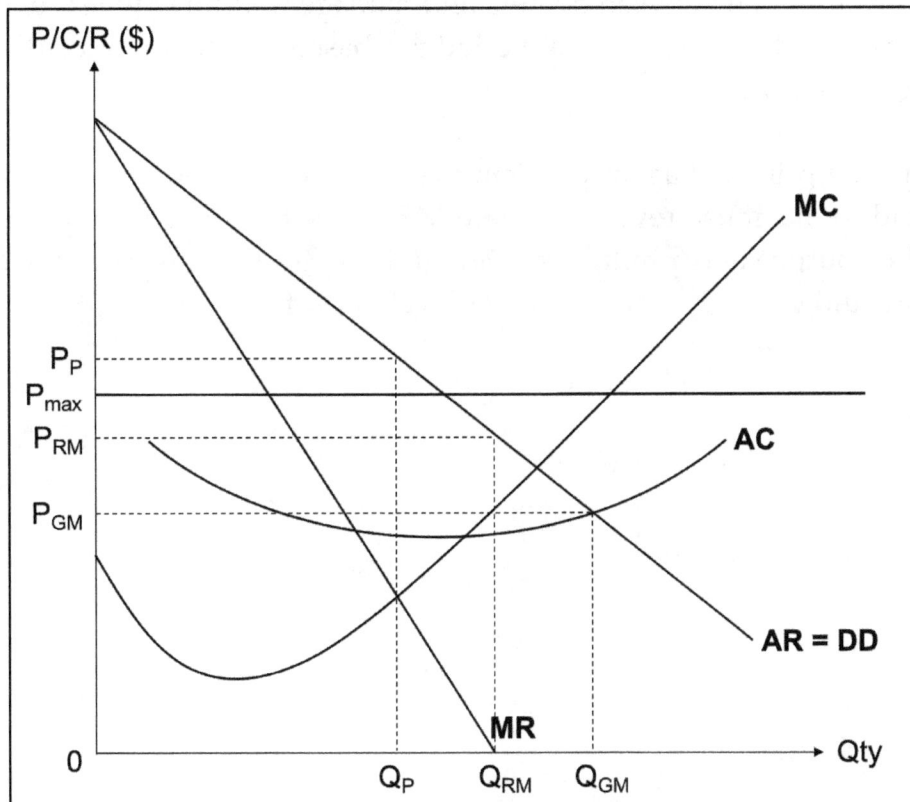

Fig. 26. Conditions under which a firm cannot or does not maximise profit.

7. One good example would be a maximum price, that may be set at Pmax (as shown in Fig. 26 on the previous page) which is below the profit maximising price (P_P). Firms are thus forced by legislation to sell no higher than Pmax and earn lesser profit. (Do note that there will be a new profit maximising equilibrium under this regulatory condition. Hence, to some extent, the firm can still profit maximise within the constraints of Pmax, but it will be lesser than the maximum amount of profits it could have earned without the price ceiling.)

8. In addition, firms may not be willing to maximise profits as they may have alternate objectives other than profit maximisation.

9. One would be growth maximisation, where the firm focuses on maximising quantity to increase market share, and as such may produce at maximum output level while still making normal profit, like at Q_{GM} and pricing at P_{GM} as shown in Fig. 26.

10. In addition, firms may also choose to commit to corporate social responsibility (CSR) and spend on projects in order to achieve a favourable public image. This can lead to higher costs and lower profits.

11. Firms may also be plagued with differences in objectives, especially if there is a significant divide between owners and managers. While owners expect profits to be maximised, managers may be judged based on the amount of revenue they bring to the firm.

12. As such, a principal agent problem may arise where the managers choose to opt instead to maximise revenue, where MR = 0, which is not the profit maximising level of output and produce at Q_{RM} and charge P_{RM} instead as seen in Fig. 26. This would certainly lead to a lower level of profit.

Concluding Section

1. In conclusion, it must be acknowledged that firms still mostly want to maximise profits.

2. Even though there may be alternate objectives, there is often still the aim to maximise profits in the long term.

3. Growth maximisation for example can allow the firm to maximise the profits in the long term with increased market share and the reaping of more internal economies of scale and hence cost advantages.

4. Conducting CSR can also build brand loyalty from the good reputation of the firm, allowing greater price setting ability and thus higher revenues in the future.

5. However, firms may not be fully able maximise their profits.

6. How close a firms are to profit maximising depends on the extent of information available, and the presence of government intervention.

18. Discuss whether the Internet has made markets more perfect. (15)

Introduction

1. A market that is "more perfect" is one that more closely resembles a Perfectly Competitive (PC) market.

2. The PC market has several key characteristics – an infinite number of buyers and sellers; perfect information; free entry and exit of firms and homogenous goods.

Thesis 1: Lowered Barriers to Entry

1. The internet has drastically lowered the barriers to entry (hindrances that prevent or discourage prospective firms) for many markets.

2. The start-up costs for establishing an online store are significantly lower than a brick-and-mortar store. There is no need to pay rent for a physical shopfront and labour costs are reduced due to lowered manpower requirements (for instance, retail positions like that of cashiers are no longer needed in an online store).

3. Furthermore, it is extremely simple to set up an online store. Many websites exist for the sole purpose of serving as a platform through which sellers can sell goods online. These range from global platforms like Amazon or eBay, to ones that are more niche and serve smaller markets, like Carousell that operates in Singapore. There are also companies, like Wix and SquareSpace, which allows sellers to create their own dedicated website with e-payment services – without the need for any knowledge of coding. It merely takes a few 'clicks' to get an online store up and running.

4. Thus, barriers to entry have been lowered, allowing for many more sellers in the market. The market also now more closely resemble the characteristic of free entry and exit of firms and hence it is more perfect.

Thesis 2: Global Marketplace

1. The internet has also brought together a global marketplace. Increased interconnectivity now allows buyers to connect with sellers around the world with virtually no geographical restrictions in place.

2. For example, Zelos is a Singapore-based start-up that makes and sells watches. While it only has physical shopfronts in Singapore, it has used Internet retail platforms to sell watches to a global audience, including Americans and Europeans. Owing to the internet, Zelos is now able to enter the American and European markets whereas previously it would have been limited to only the Singaporean market.

3. The number of sellers and buyers in every market has now increased dramatically. Hence, the market is more perfect.

Thesis 3: Increased Access to Information

1. The internet has also increased buyers' and sellers' access to information. With the internet facilitating the explosion and exchange of information, many sellers are able to 'copy' ideas of each other and learn new methods of production quite quickly.

2. Similarly, the internet has also allowed buyers to easily compare different products online, from their price to their perceived quality. Buyers can have all the information at hand when they make a decision to purchase a particular product over another. There are also portals like Trip.com that allow easy comparison of flights and hotel prices and services.

3. All in all, the Internet now allows for information to be more accessible to buyers and sellers alike, allowing markets to become more perfect.

Anti-Thesis 1: Large firms can still dominate

1. Large firms have the financial resources to tap into more advanced, more highly-specialised technologies, exploiting the use of the internet to increase their market share. Such firms are also able to spread out the IT costs incurred over a greater number of output, reducing the cost per unit output.

2. For example, large companies could employ AI technologies to better analyse preferences of buyers and their online behaviour, allowing them to come up with products and offers that better appeal to consumers. These can be costly investments, which smaller firms would be unable to engage in and lack the scale to achieve a lower average cost.

3. Due to their resources and the economies of scale, large firms may also be able to dominate online advertising, for example, through paying for many banner ads and on more prominent spots. This can result in small firms being drowned out by the advertising bombardment of large firms.

4. As a result, large firms remain dominant, both in the physical as well as online and the markets remain imperfect.

Anti-Thesis 2: Internet-based Monopolies

1. The rise of the internet technology has also facilitated the creation of technological behemoths, effectively internet-based monopolies in the newly-emerged markets in which they operate. One example is Google, which is the dominant search engine in the world, holding 92% market share. It has become so dominant that the word "google" is now synonymous with "searching for something online". This has allowed Google to be virtually a monopoly over online advertising. Amazon is also a near-monopoly over book sales online.

2. As the internet has led to such new monopolies, it has not made markets more perfect.

Anti-Thesis 3 : High Barriers to Entry still exist

1. The internet has not been able to reduce the barriers to entry for all industries.

2. For example, industries with high capital outlay like the shipping industry, which relies on an immense amount of physical capital (large freight ships to move cargo between countries). The rise of the internet has not changed the fact that an immense start-up capital is needed to acquire such physical capital in order for a shipping company to be established.

3. Therefore, in such markets, the internet has not made them more perfect.

Concluding Section

1. The internet has indeed made certain markets more perfect, specifically retail markets boosted by the rise of e-commerce.

2. However, this cannot be said for all markets concerned. Only industries where production methods have been simplified thanks to internet technologies, do we find more perfect markets. In others, the internet has little to no effect on production activities at all, and does not make the markets concerned more perfect. The internet also gives rise to new industries and markets, such as social media, where monopolies have formed.

19. Explain how a rise in GST impacts consumer expenditure on different types of goods and services. (10)

Introduction

1. Consumer expenditure is the amount spent by consumers to purchase a good or service, and is calculated by taking the product of price and quantity bought.

2. GST is an indirect tax, often levied as a percentage of the good's retail price.

3. As GST changes, the market equilibrium will be affected, causing consumer expenditure to change as well. The effect on the market equilibrium can be determined via demand and supply interactions.

4. Demand refers to the quantity of a good or service that consumers are willing and able to purchase at various prices over a fixed period of time, ceteris paribus. Supply refers to the quantity of a good or service that firms are willing and able to produce at various prices over a fixed period of time, ceteris paribus.

Effect of the tax

1. The increase in GST leads to an increase in the unit cost of production of firms, leading to a fall in profit margins for producers, thereby disincentivising them from producing. Supply falls, as depicted in Fig. 27 below, from S to S + new tax.

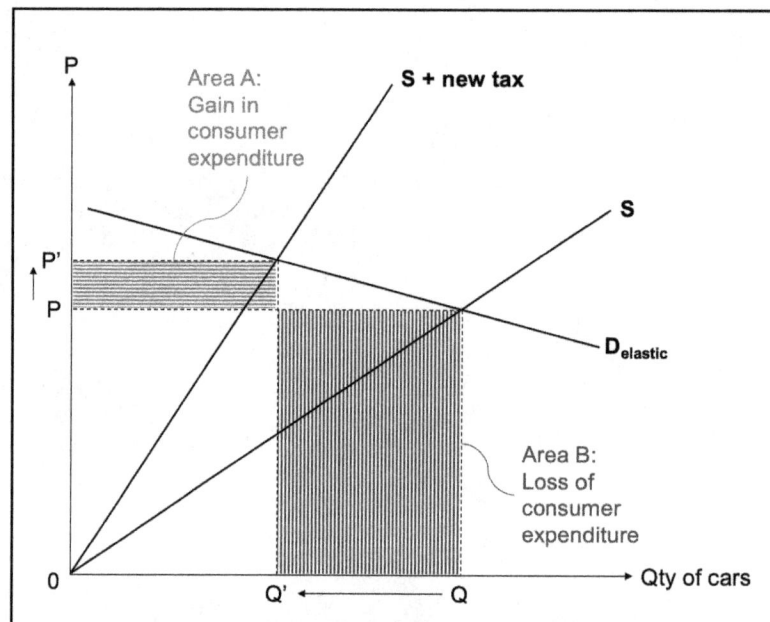

Fig. 27. Impact of GST on CE when Dd is price-elastic.

2. Note that the shift of the supply curve is pivotal, since the GST is levied in terms of percentage of the good's price – thus a greater tax amount occurs at a higher price along the supply curve.

3. The decrease in supply causes a shortage to exist at the original equilibrium price P. This shortage places an upward pressure on price. As prices increase, quantity demanded falls and quantity supplied rises, eventually resulting at a new market equilibrium at a higher price P' and a lower quantity Q', wherein the shortage is eliminated.

4. The new consumer expenditure following the imposition of the tax is given by the product of P' and Q'.

5. The effect of the tax on consumer expenditure varies based on the price elasticity of demand of the goods in question.

6. Price Elasticity of Demand measures the responsiveness of the quantity demanded for a good to changes in its price, ceteris paribus.

Case 1: PED > 1

7. The demand for luxury goods tend to be price elastic. This is because such goods are not necessary and also tend to constitute a large proportion of income due to their high price tag. Examples of luxury goods include cars and jewelry.

8. As seen in Fig. 27, the gain in consumer expenditure owing to increased prices is represented by area A, while the loss in consumer expenditure due to reduced quantity consumed is represented by area B.

9. Since the demand for cars is price elastic, the quantity demanded falls by a greater amount than the rise in price, causing area A to be greater than area B. Consequently, in mathematical terms, P x Q > P' x Q', and consumer expenditure falls.

Case 2: PED < 1

1. The demand for necessity-type goods tend to be price inelastic. Such goods are often staple items, for which there exist few available substitutes, and the items are deemed as necessary for survival. Examples of necessities include rice in Asian countries, electricity etc.

2. Addictive goods also exhibit similar characteristics; their demand is price inelastic. Addicts deem such goods as a strict 'necessity' to them. Examples include cigarettes for smokers and alcohol for alcoholics.

3. Examining the market for rice below, upon implementation of the increased GST, the decrease in supply causes a shift along the demand curve for rice. As a result, the quantity of rice consumed decreases less than proportionately to the increase in the price of rice. This can be seen from Fig. 28 below.

4. The gain in consumer expenditure on rice owing to increased prices is represented by area A, while the loss in consumer expenditure due to reduced quantity consumed is represented by area B. Since the demand for rice is price inelastic, the quantity demanded falls by a smaller extent than the price increase, causing area B to be greater than area A. Consequently, in mathematical terms, P′ x Q′ > P x Q, and consumer expenditure rises.

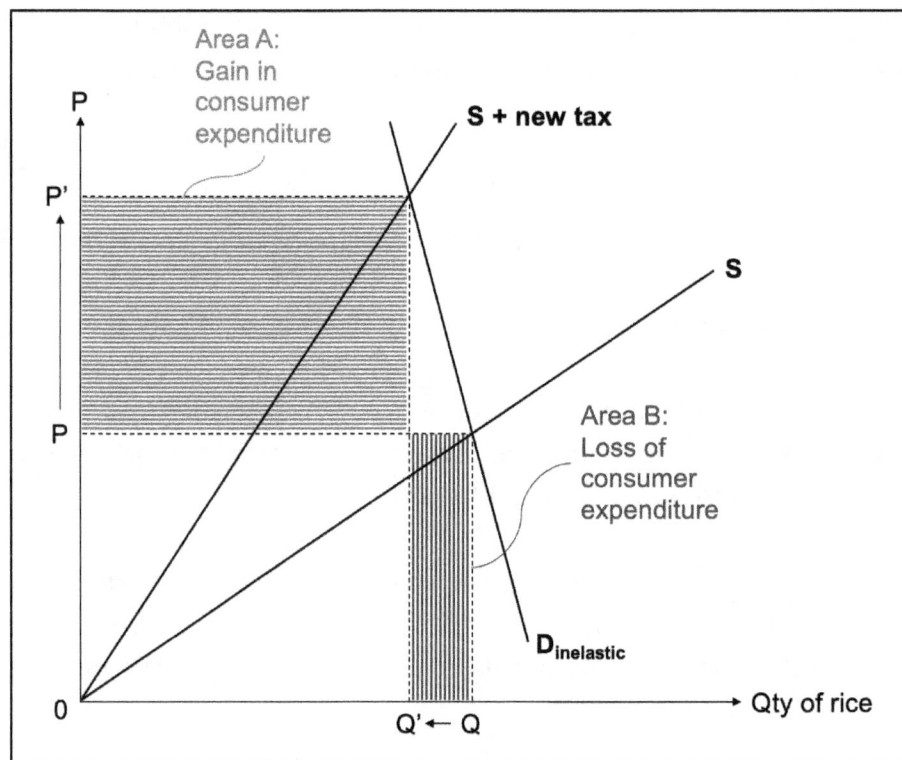

Fig. 28. Impact of GST on CE when Dd is price-inelastic.

<u>Effect on related markets</u>

1. However, it is important to understand the context in which GST is levied. In Singapore, the government only levies the GST on goods and services sold by businesses earning more than SGD 1 million in revenue per year.

2. Small business, such as street food hawkers, would continue selling their goods without the GST being levied, and could therefore see an increase in demand for their products.

3. This is because substitutes like cafe food may now become pricier due to the hike in GST, which may encourage some consumers to switch to consuming more hawker food.

4. The increase in demand would increase both equilibrium price and quantity sold, thus increasing consumer expenditure.

20. Discuss whether the combined effect of a rise in incomes and a rise in GST is likely to cause the quantities transacted of different types of goods and services to rise or fall. (15)

Introduction

1. A rise in incomes means that households are able to enjoy higher purchasing power.

2. The effect of a rise in income on the demand for a good, depends on the income-elasticity of demand (YED) value of the said good.

3. YED measures the responsiveness of demand for a good to a change in income, ceteris paribus.

Case 1: Positive YED

1. Normal goods see their demand increase given an increase in income, thereby having a positive YED.

2. However, the extent of YED varies.

3. For normal-necessities, their demand increases less-than-proportionately for a given increase in income.

4. On the other hand, the demand for luxury goods increases more than proportionately.

5. Ceteris paribus, the increase in demand would cause the quantities transacted of normal goods to increase.

6. As explained previously in Essay #19, an increase in GST would cause a decrease in supply. Ceteris paribus, this decrease in supply would reduce the quantities transacted of all non-tax-exempt goods and services.

7. Therefore, the resultant effect on quantity would vary depending on the extent of the increase in GST, the extent of the increase in income, the magnitude of YED, and the magnitude of PED.

<u>Case 1a) YED value between 0 and 1</u>

8. For normal necessities with a YED value between 0 and 1, any increases in income would lead to less significant increases in demand. Therefore, it is likely that demand would not increase to a significant-enough extent to make up for the falling supply, barring any huge increases in income.

9. However, the demand for normal necessities might be highly price inelastic. This is especially true for essential daily items, like electricity and staple foods like rice.

10. Thus, quantity demanded falls less than proportionately to an increase in price, ceteris paribus.

11. Therefore, an increase in GST would only reduce the quantities transacted of such goods by a small extent, as illustrated in Essay #19.

12. Increases in income could possibly see demand rising enough to overcome the decreases in quantity due to the GST rise and thus there could be no change in quantities transacted as illustrated in Fig. 29 below.

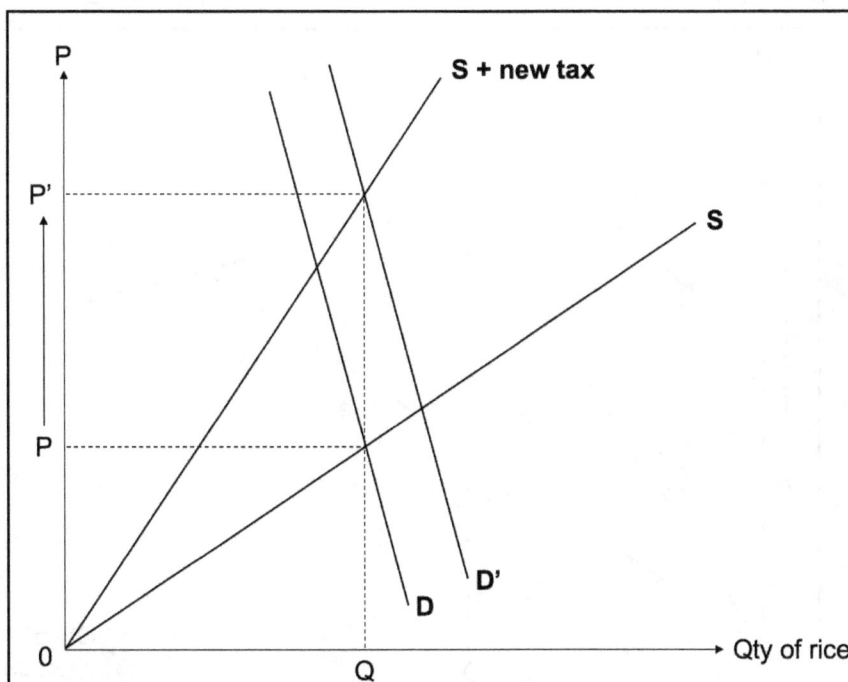

Fig. 29. No change in Quantity transacted for Normal-Necessity.

13. The exact outcome would also depend on the extent of rise in income versus rise in GST rates.

<u>Case 1b) YED value greater than 1</u>

14. For luxury goods with a YED value above 1, increases in income would lead to large jumps in demand. As a result, it is likely that demand would increase very significantly, exceeding the decreases in supply owing to the higher GST.

15. However, the demand for luxury goods is likely to be price elastic. Luxury items, such as sport cars or jewelry, take up a high proportion of income and are inherently non-essential.

16. Therefore, an increase in GST may also greatly reduce the quantities transacted of luxury items, as illustrated in Essay #19.

17. However, with a rise in income, the spending on the good would become a smaller proportion of the higher income and thus PED values may become lower.

18. Overall, there will likely be some net increase in quantities transacted as illustrated in Fig. 30 below.

19. The exact outcome would also depend on the extent of rise in income versus rise in GST rates as well as the exact values of PED and YED.

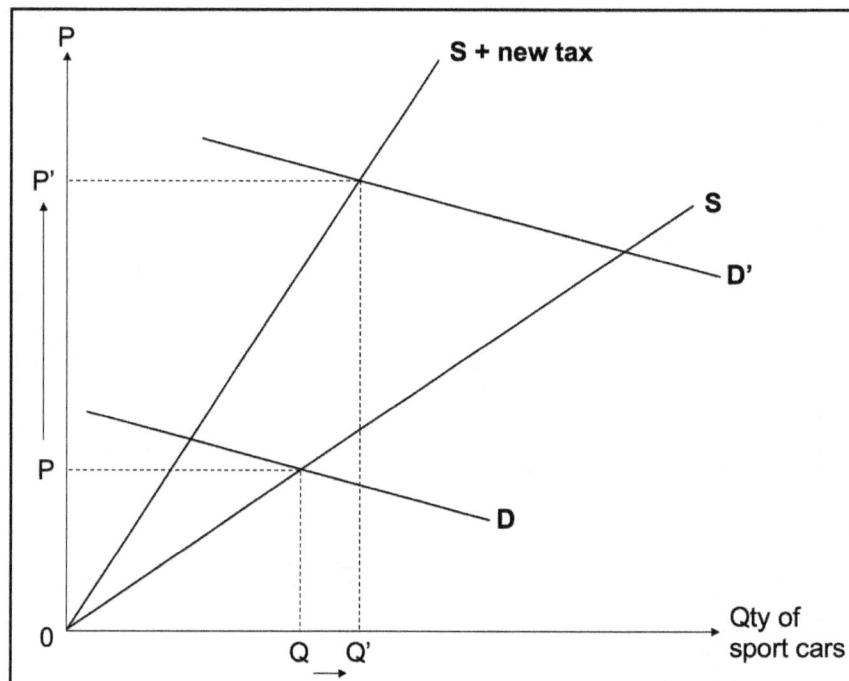

Fig. 30. Slight Increase in Quantity transacted for Normal-Luxury.

Case 2: Negative YED

1. Goods whose demand decreases given an increase in income are termed as 'inferior goods' with a YED value that is negative. Given a choice, consumers would rather purchase higher-quality substitutes to such goods. Examples of inferior goods include instant noodles.

2. With a rise in incomes, consumers would have increased purchasing power at their disposal. This would enable consumers to now afford the more preferred substitutes to these inferior goods. Consequently, the demand for inferior goods will decrease.

3. At the same time, the increase in GST would entail a reduction in the supply of the inferior goods.

4. With a decrease in both demand and supply, the result is clear cut. The quantity transacted of inferior goods will decrease as seen in Fig. 31.

5. The decrease is likely to be quite significant as PED is expected to be high give the availability of substitutes.

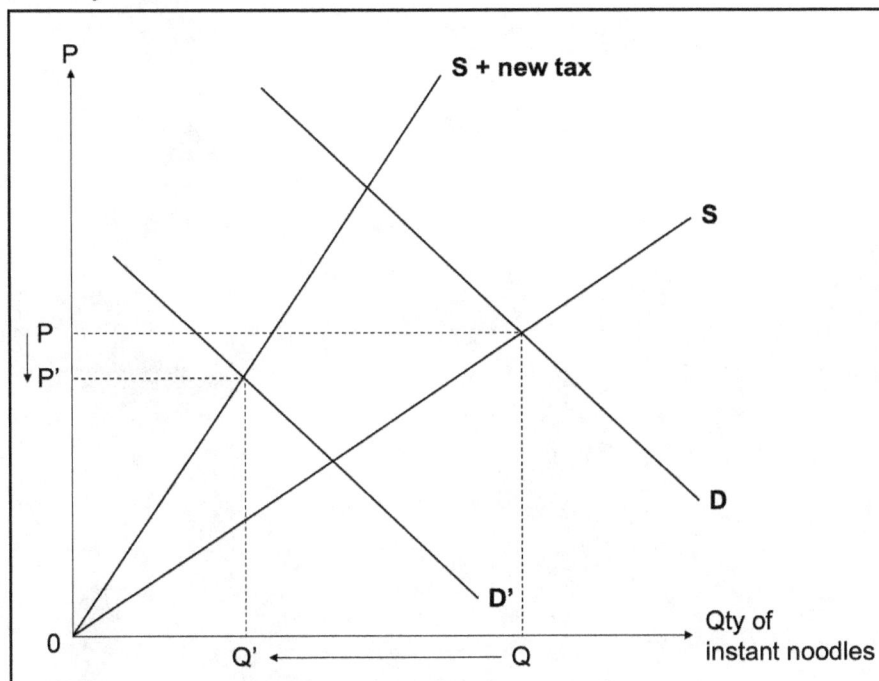

Fig. 31. Fall in Quantity transacted for Inferior Good.

<u>Concluding Section</u>

1. Thus, the most important factor affecting quantity transacted is the nature of the good concerned, which would affect its PED and YED value.

2. In general, we expect quantities transacted to increase for luxury goods, stay about the same for necessities and fall for inferior goods.

3. The extent of the GST hike and extent of increase in income would also be important to know in order to determine how the quantity transacted would most likely change for the various normal goods.

4. The above analysis also assumes that producers will hike the price in order to pass on some tax burden to consumers.

5. However, in some highly competitive markets as well as in oligopolistic markets, producers may not do so and hence the change in quantity transacted would follow the direction of change in demand due to rising income.

www.ingramcontent.com/pod-product-compliance
Lightning Source LLC
Chambersburg PA
CBHW051229200326
41519CB00025B/7311